BRIGADISTA
Harvest and War in Nicaragua

edited by

Jeff Jones

Eyewitness Accounts of North American Volunteers
Working in Nicaragua

PRAEGER

PRAEGER SPECIAL STUDIES • PRAEGER SCIENTIFIC

New York • Philadelphia • Eastbourne, UK
Toronto • Hong Kong • Tokyo • Sydney

Library of Congress Cataloging-in-Publication Data
Main entry under title:

Brigadista : harvest and war in Nicaragua.

Includes index.
1. Nicaragua – History – Revolution, 1979 – Influence.
2. Voluntarism – United States. 3. Voluntarism –
Nicaragua. I. Jones, Jeffrey.
F1528.B75 1986   972.85'053   85-24384
ISBN 0-03-005213-0 (alk. paper)
ISBN 0-03-005214-9 (pbk. : alk. paper)

Published in 1986 by Praeger Publishers
CBS Educational and Professional Publishing, a Division of CBS Inc.
521 Fifth Avenue, New York, NY 10175 USA

6789 052 987654321

Printed in the United States of America on acid-free paper

INTERNATIONAL OFFICES

Orders from outside the United States should be sent to the appropriate address listed below. Orders from areas not
listed below should be placed through CBS International Publishing, 383 Madison Ave., New York, NY 10175 USA

Australia, New Zealand
Holt Saunders, Pty, Ltd., 9 Waltham St., Artarmon, N.S.W. 2064, Sydney, Australia

Canada
Holt, Rinehart & Winston of Canada, 55 Horner Ave., Toronto, Ontario, Canada M8Z 4X6

Europe, the Middle East, & Africa
Holt Saunders, Ltd., 1 St. Anne's Road, Eastbourne, East Sussex, England BN21 3UN

Japan
Holt Saunders, Ltd., Ichibancho Central Building, 22-1 Ichibancho, 3rd Floor, Chiyodaku, Tokyo, Japan

Hong Kong, Southeast Asia
Holt Saunders Asia, Ltd., 10 Fl, Intercontinental Plaza, 94 Granville Road, Tsim Sha Tsui East, Kowloon,
Hong Kong

**Manuscript submissions should be sent to the Editorial Director, Praeger Publishers, 521 Fifth Avenue,
New York, NY 10175 USA**

Tell the North American people that I send them greetings; that the doors of Nicaragua are open to all those who want to come to work.... You can tell the North American readers that I have been facing the United States for many years, bound by the greatest duty to defend the autonomy of Nicaragua, but that I hold toward its people neither rancor nor hatred.

Augusto Cesar Sandino
1928

To Carroll Ishee

"*Perhaps my greatest fear has been the prospect of wasting away on the sidelines, exiled from history, isolated from the processes which represent the possibility of human dignity.*"

Carroll Ishee was born in Philadelphia, Mississippi, on September 29, 1953. He was an active opponent of the U.S. war against Vietnam and worked hard in support of the African colonies fighting for their liberation in the mid-1970s. In 1981, he left his family and journeyed to El Salvador. He became a militant of the Faribundo Marti National Liberation Front of El Salvador, fighting under the name "Carlos." In August 1983, he was killed in combat in Morazan Province, El Salvador, by fire from a U.S.-supplied Huey helicopter.

Appreciation

A book such as this, with more than sixty different voices, naturally required many gracious acts of assistance and cooperation. Those who made this book possible were the Nicaraguan people who fought and won, and the North Americans who answered the Nicaraguan call for assistance and friendship.

This book could not have been done without Sara Miles and Corinne Rafferty of the Nicaragua Exchange staff. They were both generous and critical friends. Eleanore and Michael Kennedy made special efforts to help with introductions and ideas. So did Michael Ratner, Julie Light, and Joel Lefkowitz.

I want to thank LeVaun Ishee and Nell Ishee for sharing part of their lives.

Anne Geismar was the first to read the manuscript and say, "This is a book." Suzanne Sangree contributed both her brigade experience and her skill as a translator, as did Jan Perlin. Tesi Kohlenberg and Dina Micklin Silver were supportive friends. Evelyn Wiener, who demonstrated in support of Sandino in the 1920s, shared her wisdom, her unfailing optimism, and her typewriter.

Margarita Clark and Sofia Clark helped, as did Rosa Marina Zelaya, Jorge Samper Blanco, and staff members from the CNSP in Managua.

Warmest regards to Lynda Sharp at Praeger, who had the idea for this book and gave me the opportunity to create it.

Special feelings of love go to Eleanor and Thai, for writing me poems and taking care of Arthur Lares while I was in Nicaragua.

Contents

Foreword

In 1936, the people of Spain cast their ballots in an election that brought to power a coalition of working class and liberal parties. It was a great day for the majority of the Spanish people. The winning coalition ran on a pledge of distributing land to the farmers, jobs for the jobless, hospitals for the ill, free schools and education for everyone, women's rights, and the separation of church from state. It was a new beginning for a people whose desires for a better life had too long been suppressed.

The election victory had special significance. In Europe, Hitler and his Nazi philosophy were on the march, growing stronger and bolder each day. Yet few countries outside of the Soviet Union were offering any programs to stop the spread of Nazism. In the minds and hearts of progressive people throughout the world, the Spanish election victory had resulted in an uplifting of spirits.

Then came July 18. Five months after the elections, General Franco, with the blessings of Hitler and Mussolini, led his army command in a revolt against the democratically elected government. Before the exultant republic could consolidate its newly won victory, the hand of Spanish fascism struck!

If the revolt came as a surprise to the republic, what came after was just as devastating. First, England refused to sell defense materiel to Spain; then France closed tight her borders, allowing no help to cross over. But the republic thought they had an ace in the hole. Surely the United States would not turn her back on a sister democracy now in deep trouble.

But the United States *did* turn its back on republican Spain by quickly enacting a nonintervention act, banning the sale of arms to either side. Spain soon learned that yesterday's friends would not necessarily stand by her and that nations born in struggle do not always lend a sympathetic hand to other democratic countries in trouble. Ironically, it was not Franco who was pleading for arms. He had all he could handle, supplied by Hitler and Mussolini. It was not Franco that the U.S. nonintervention policy was hurting but the young republic, the arsenals of which had been stripped bare by Franco.

As the well-armed fascists moved closer to the gates of Madrid, a plea went out from the people of Spain, calling on all those who cherished democracy and hated fascism to join with them in routing the invaders from Spanish soil.

It was this call for help that brought over 40,000 men and women from all continents to the front lines in Spain. There were many obstacles to be overcome to reach Spain, but, in spite of the barriers, the call for help was answered. Among the volunteers were some 3,200 U.S. citizens, half of whom would die in battle. We were school teachers, seamen, longshoremen, doctors, nurses, teamsters, clerks, students, and men and women from many other professions.

The volunteers were proving to the Spanish people that they were *not* alone in their fight to safeguard their democracy. The North Americans were also telling the Spanish people by example that they did *not* agree with their government's position of imposing an embargo on arms to Spain.

The war in Spain ended with the defeat of the republic. Six months after the fascists took control, World War II broke out. The United States, which had failed to support Spanish democracy, would now find itself locked in battle, face to face with the fascist armies. Europe became pockmarked with the gravesites of U.S. citizens killed in the effort to defeat and destroy fascism.

Today, forty-five years later, there is a parallel to the Spanish struggle. The people of Nicaragua, having ousted the brutal dictatorship of Somoza and having set up their own duly elected democratic government, are now faced with the fact that the Reagan administration is supporting a movement to overthrow their government by force.

The CIA is deeply involved in leading and sustaining the contras. Their purpose is to disrupt the normal routine of the country, to burn and destroy its crops, to sabotage its industries, to kill and maim its leaders, and to bring the country to its knees—then return it to the old days of a dictatorship of tyrants. Millions of dollars are being supplied by the United States and its allies to arm and support the contras, an army composed of followers of the former dictator Somoza and other mercenaries who hunger for the thrill of raping, looting, killing, and destroying.

Today we find hundreds of women and men who are appalled and disgusted with the present murderous policy of our government. Like us, the men and women who volunteered to go to Spain and assist that democratic cause, they are eager to volunteer their services to the people of Nicaragua in whatever manner they know how, be it harvesting the coffee crop, picking cotton, or assisting in the construction and repair of houses for the people.

This has been the constructive answer of many North Americans. This effort to create, to build, to share, to transmit love and concern to each other is contrary to the administration's policy of permitting and financing murder, destruction, and hopelessness. It is the act of reaching out, telling the Nicaraguan people that *not* all North Americans are in agreement with the administration's policy.

I feel a deep sense of pride knowing that my fellow men and women have accepted the challenge to defy the administration's policy of hostility toward a friendly people, by going to Nicaragua and helping a people fulfill their dreams and hopes for a productive country that answers their needs. It is with this loving feeling that we read of the experiences of some of the volunteers who have taken their labors of love to a nation many miles away. As they come home, they bring with them first-hand knowledge of a nation that is placing its hopes on the decency and understanding of the people of the United States to work with them, not against them.

It is rewarding and nurtures the spirit to know that there are people who care enough to make and fulfill a commitment. One day we all shall live in peace and good fellowship. Toward achieving that end, the good fight will go on. May the love of the people who wrote their stories rub off on all of us so we can be inspired to work harder for peace and understanding, so that the people of Nicaragua can fulfill their destiny, too, by living in their country surrounded by love and friendship and knowing that they have nothing to fear.

May you be enriched by the stories you are about to read.

Bill Bailey
Veteran, Abraham Lincoln Brigades
San Francisco, California

Preface

I've had my share of coffee. But I knew nothing of what it took to bring that coffee to my morning table until February 1985, when I joined seventy-four other North Americans on a volunteer work brigade to Nicaragua.

There is something about physical labor that demands honesty. Idealized notions about sunup to sundown rural work and poverty slipped from my mind as I stood with the other brigadistas outside the barn that was to be our home for the next three weeks.

On the fertile slopes of the Masaya volcano, twenty-eight kilometers south of Managua, we worked with Nicaraguan students and campesinos, picking the trees clean in the final weeks of the harvest. Under the jungle canopy was a mingling of voices, Spanish and English—a sound that stays with me.

This book is a mingling of voices, a collection of brigadista experiences from North Americans who worked in the harvests, in construction, in cultural centers, and on reforestation projects. It is as varied and as broad-based as the brigadista movement itself; as diverse as the many ways in which solidarity with Nicaragua becomes real.

Understanding and sharing in the Nicaraguan revolutionary process has been for me, as it is for most brigadistas, a deeply moving experience. I remember the sense of joy and pride I felt as I was leaving the coffee farm where we had been working. The tears that came were an expression of a couple of feelings: concern for the future of the campesino families and students with whom we had lived and worked; and pride in my fellow North Americans, who had made such adjustments from our world of privilege and material wealth. We had done what we came to do: we had learned, we had shared, we had contributed.

I do not pretend to be a neutral observer of events in Central America. I am a veteran of the Vietnam antiwar movement and a partisan of the liberation of the human spirit from exploitation. The Sandinista Revolution in Nicaragua seems to me the most profound and positive event to occur in our hemisphere in a quarter-century. I believe it is in our interest as a people to work for its survival. In the tradition of the Abraham Lincoln Brigades, of the Mississippi Freedom Summer, and of the internationalists who fought with Sandino in the 1920s, these brigades to Nicaragua continue: they are our way of reaching for the best in our own nation's history.

Jeff Jones
New York City
March 1985

Spanish Words and Abbreviations

AMNLAE—Asociación Mujeres Nicaragüense, Luisa Amanda Espinosa. The Luisa Amanda Espinosa Association of Nicaraguan Women. National women's organization named in honor of the first woman to die in armed combat against Somoza.

ATC—Asociación de Trabajadores del Campo. Agricultural Workers Union.

barrio—an urban neighborhood.

CDS—Comité Defensa Sandinista. Community-based defense committees.

CNE—Casa Nicaragüense de Español. Nicaraguan House of Spanish, a language school.

CNSP—Comité Nicaragüense de Solidaridad Con Los Pueblos. National Committee in Solidarity with the Peoples. Nicaraguan organization with responsibility for organizing the international work brigades.

consignas—political slogans chanted in a call and response fashion.

empresa—groups of UPEs and other farms organized regionally under government auspices.

EPS—Ejército Popular Sandinista. Sandinista Popular Army.

FSLN—Frente Sandinista Liberación Nacional. Sandinista National Liberation Front.

IRENA—Instituto de Recursos Naturales. Nicaraguan Institute for Natural Resources and the Environment.

militante—political activist. In Nicaragua, a member or supporter of the Sandinista party.

responsable—person in charge, with responsibility for welfare and actions of others. Used by brigadistas to refer to North American leaders and medical personnel, as well as Nicaraguans with responsibility for the brigades.

UNAG—Unión Nicaragüense de Agricultures y Ganaderos. Union of Small Agricultural Producers and Ranchers.

UPE—Unidad Producción Estatal. State Production Unit. A farm administered under the auspices of the government. UPEs are sometimes referred to as haciendas or fincas.

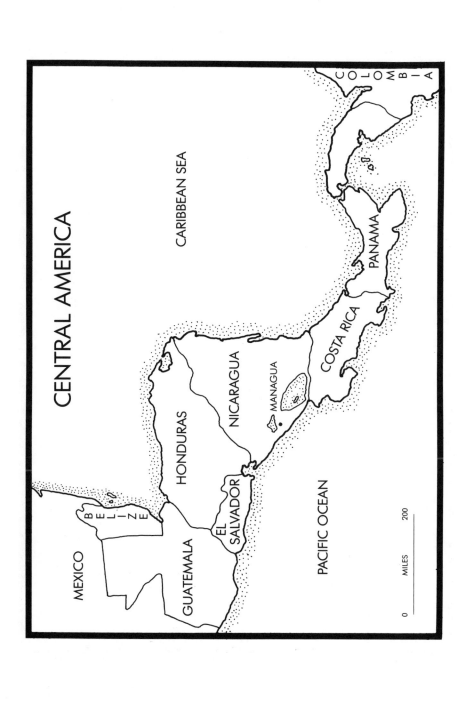

CENTRAL AMERICA

MEXICO

BELIZE

GUATEMALA

EL SALVADOR

HONDURAS

NICARAGUA

MANAGUA

COSTA RICA

PANAMA

COLOMBIA

CARIBBEAN SEA

PACIFIC OCEAN

0   200
MILES

REPUBLIC OF NICARAGUA

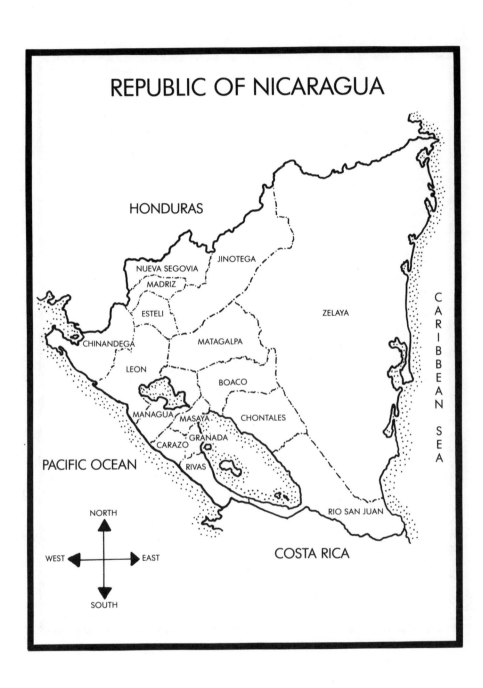

HONDURAS

NUEVA SEGOVIA

MADRIZ

JINOTEGA

ESTELI

ZELAYA

CHINANDEGA

MATAGALPA

LEON

BOACO

MANAGUA   MASAYA

CHONTALES

CARAZO   GRANADA

PACIFIC OCEAN

RIVAS

RIO SAN JUAN

COSTA RICA

CARIBBEAN SEA

NORTH

WEST   EAST

SOUTH

REPUBLIC OF NICARAGUA

HONDURAS

RIO COCO

RIO COCO

WASPAN

PUERTO CABEZAS

8

OCOTAL 4 22

6 SOMOTO

SAN LORENZO

15

23 17 5

GOLFO DE FONSECA

ESTELI

JINOTEGA

19 18 3
1

MATAGALPA
16

RIO GRANDE DE MATAGALPA

C
A
R
I
B
B
E
A
N

CHINANDEGA

13

CORINTO

LEON 21

10

BOACO

S
E
A

PUERTO SANDINO

MANAGUA

LA LIBERTAD

RAMA

EL CRUCERO

11

JUIGALPA

BLUEFIELDS

POCHOMIL

14 12
9 7

LAGO DE NICARAGUA

20

SAN MIGUELITO
2 MORRILLO
SAN CARLOS

PACIFIC OCEAN

COSTA RICA

RIO SAN JUAN

KEY

1	APASCALI
2	ARCHIPIELAGO DE SOLENTINAME
3	COSIQUINA
4	EL CHIPOTE
5	EL CUA
6	EL ESPINO
7	GRANADA
8	JALAPA
9	JINOTEPE
10	LAGO DE MANAGUA
11	MASAYA
12	MONIMBO
13	MUY MUY
14	NIQUINOHOMO
15	PALACAQUINA
16	PANCASAN
17	PANTASMA
18	POTOSi
19	PUNTA NATA
20	RIVAS
21	VOLCAN MOMOTOMBO
22	WIWILI
23	YALI

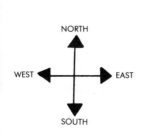

NORTH

WEST EAST

SOUTH

Introduction

On July 19, 1984, Comandante Daniel Ortega addressed the crowds celebrating the fifth anniversary of Nicaragua's Revolution and sent a "combative embrace" to the people of the world who have helped Nicaragua, "especially the people of the United States." Ortega's declaration to us that "this revolution is also yours" reflects more than Nicaragua's generosity: it acknowledges the special role that internacionalistas have played in this extremely nationalistic revolution, from the time of Sandino on.

Thousands of volunteers, largely from Western Europe and Cuba, have participated in the reconstruction of Nicaragua since the triumph in 1979, working as teachers, agricultural specialists, doctors, and technicians. Almost a third of the faculty in Nicaragua's university system is made up of internacionalistas; North American, French, Soviet, and Cuban health workers help staff clinics and hospitals throughout the country. These permanent residents, including hundreds of religious workers from all over the world, are increasingly joined by brigadistas—international volunteers who work in short-term projects where the need is greatest.

In 1983 to 1984, 1,575 volunteers from the United States, Italy, Germany, France, Mexico, Scandinavia, and Latin America responded to a call for assistance with Nicaragua's vital coffee and cotton harvests, endangered by the contra war. By far, the largest contingent came from the United States, under the sponsorship of the National Network in Solidarity with the Nicaraguan People. Over 650 U.S. volunteers worked side by side with Nicaraguan campesinos, picking coffee and cotton from December 1983 through February 1984. From across the country, citizens formed brigades, offering their concrete support to the Nicaraguan people in a "harvest of peace."

Brigadistas from these first harvest groups found that their real work began when they returned to the United States. As one U.S. brigadista wrote, "We learned to have a sense of pride and deep responsibility about the word internacionalista." Some of them became founders of such smaller, technically skilled groups as the construction brigade that would return to Nicaragua to build a community center. Others became activists in the growing solidarity movement in the United States, determined to spread the word about the U.S. war in Central America. A newsletter—*The Brigadista Bulletin*[1]—was started, uniting brigadistas around the country; a film—"Harvest of Peace"[2]—was made; local groups of brigadistas raised funds for material aid to Nicaragua, organized publicity campaigns, and marched with veterans of the Abraham Lincoln Brigades in protest against the administration's policies. By the fall of 1984, the brigades had become one of the most visible—and concrete—signs of domestic opposition to the war against Nicaragua.

---

[1]*The Brigadista Bulletin* is published by Nicaragua Exchange, a project of the Interreligious Foundation for Community Organization (IFCO). A subscription is $8.00 a year. The address is: 239 Centre Street, New York, New York 10013.

[2]"Harvest of Peace," directed by Robbie Leppzer and produced by Lisa Berger, is available from Turning Tide Productions, P.O. Box 1008, Amherst, Massachusetts 01004.

BRIGADISTA

Sara Miles

talking nicaragua

I

After the revolution Juan still
yelled at his kids
not always
just when he was trying to sleep and they
ran out banging the door

Isabel
still couldn't get the faucet to stop dripping

Elena's feet were killing her
still

everything went on the same
only different after the revolution:
the same
only different.

II

The kind and very blond
American actress wants to know about Nicaragua.
She thinks the problem must be
economic: "What do they have? What's there
that the United States needs?"

"Talking Nicaragua" by Sara Miles has also appeared in *Native Dancer*, Curbstone Press, 1985. Reprinted with permission of the author.

It's not copper, this time
not gold
and no oil, that's for sure
it's not uranium or diamonds:
what do they have?

There's a little bit of coffee
some cotton, barely enough for a shirt
There's not a lot of anything in Nicaragua
not even people
and the people are the same.

Only different.

III

"The Nicaraguans," laughs another, "they remember
everything!" And Jaime
Martin Espinoza, pale
serious
twenty-four
doesn't understand. He looks up
from the book he is holding:
"We have to remember."

And here are the photos
a high-school yearbook of the dead
ordinary faces
here are their names:
Julio Buitrago Urróz
Arlen Siu
Jesus Reyes
Enrique Campbell
page upon page and Jaime still
remembering:

"Leonel Rugama: I was eleven and Managua
was such a small town. All day

we saw the helicopters
tanks
troops trying to win against three
or four people. I remember
because that was the first time
I learned of the Frente. It took a whole army
to kill this one here. He was
a poet, you know."

Each ordinary face
a poet each
ordinary face so
very young
each ordinary face different
and dead

and still speaking saying: each face
the same.

IV

"Managua Nicaragua is a wonderful town
You can buy a hacienda for a few pesos down..."

Somoza. To say it
soured the mouth
put snakes between the teeth
whistling *you can buy a hacienda...*

With Somoza gone, it was different.

V

But it's the same
shame

New uniforms at the border but the same
lettering on the explosives

C119/LAUNCHER/MADE IN USA
only now more people can read
the labels on what comes to kill them.
The terror *MADE IN USA*
means no one there likes a bad loser
but especially everyone hates
the people who really win

something different

and plan to stay that way.

VI

What do they have?

Jaime. Elena. Juan. Isabel.
The way the lake laps liquid at the evening's knees
remembering
these living heroes
ordinary as the gritty
holy air of Nicaragua
still real despite the terror.

They have
these faces.

The same and the same
only
transformed.

HARVEST BRIGADES
December 1983–February 1984

Nica Noel Brigade, December 17–31, 1983
    harvested coffee near Estelí and Matagalpa

Ronnie Carpin Moffet Brigade, December 31, 1983–January 15, 1984
    construction, agricultural work in the area of Río San Juan, near
    the Costa Rican border

Martin Luther King Brigade, January 15–29, 1984
    harvested cotton, construction at Punta Ñata

Maura Clarke Brigade, January 29–February 14, 1984
    harvested cotton at Punta Ñata and Apascalí

February 21st Brigade, February 12–24, 1984
    harvested cotton at Apascalí and at Soledad, near León

Ric Mohr

Richard Levy

Just after sundown we arrived at El Chaquiton—a state cattle and coffee farm about twelve miles from the Honduran border. Driving in past the gates, we were met by a group of armed men and women, looking like people I had only seen in movies—but their smiles gave a warmth that I'd never seen from any soldier. About half an hour later, when we were getting set up in the dorms, a young man was among the crowd of people who came over to greet us. In conversation we learned that he was entitled to go home for Christmas, but when he heard we were coming, to make sure there was enough security, he decided to forego his vacation. What kind of a war is it where a young Nicaraguan, wearing a cut up coffee sack to keep warm because he doesn't own a coat, says he's going to stay behind and do guard duty to protect you from a group of terrorists who were created and supported by your government and sent to kill him?

Wherever we went, we were met with a great warmth, a sense of humor, and an openness to talk. Wherever we went, the fears and barriers were broken down by dancing. How distant can you feel after dancing and laughing with someone—even if he or she has a machine gun on his or her back because it's too unsafe to put it down anytime? On the first night at a welcoming ceremony, everyone started to sing the Sandinista anthem. Part way through, a murmur started going around the room. What were they going to do—here they were welcoming a group of Americans and they were fast coming up to the line in the song that calls the "Yanquis—the enemies of humanity." Seconds before the line was reached, one person, echoing everyone else's unstated thoughts said out loud, "Don't worry—they're not

Sara Miles speaking with arriving Brigadistas, Managua, Nicaragua, February, 1985. Photo by Jeff Jones.

Yanquis—they're Americans," and with a collective laugh people kept on singing at full blast.

There wasn't a single regular army soldier at El Chaquiton. But there were lots of campesinos and students walking around armed. I wondered how much trust there had to be between a government and the peasants to freely hand out machine guns to them. It couldn't happen in Guatemala or Honduras. The people we met handled the arms with a great sense of responsibility knowing that they were to defend the gains of the Revolution and not for settling personal scores. It's amazing to live under a constant reign of fear—machine guns when you eat, tell jokes, dance; patrols out to fields before you can go out to pick coffee. One Nicaraguan woman was sitting in her room when a man she didn't recognize, wearing a camouflage jacket and carrying an M-16 (and not an AK-47) walked by her room. She thought he was a contra and became hysterical.

A number of us were interested in education, so we jumped at the opportunity when a young adult education worker, visiting a friend who had volunteered as a coffee picker, offered to tell us his experiences. This eighteen-year-old teacher sat down, put his AK-47 under his legs, and began to tell us about two of his friends who had been kidnapped, tortured (fingernails pulled out, breasts cut off, raped, and castrated) and then killed by the contras. Would I be willing to take such a risk just to be a teacher? The stakes are so much higher for everything here.

After about eighteen straight meals of beans and tortillas (with rice about every third meal), I began to wonder what it would be like to eat that three times a day, every day, for the rest of my life. A lot of the campesinos made a sport of complaining about the food, but they also said that before the Revolution they rarely if ever had rice, and when times were tough there were no beans either, just dry corn tortillas and more tortillas and more tortillas.

Suzanne Marten

As I look at the conditions now, I begin to realize how horrible they must have been before the Revolution. The barrios we drove past in Managua consisted of small one or two-room shacks of scrap lumber, metal, cardboard, straw, or whatever was available. The floors are dirt, no different from the yards. And many times there isn't a door. The people share outhouses and must walk to a pump in the middle of the block for water. Their stoves are made of metal drums with fires inside and some sort of platform fixed above.

The reality of war became more tangible as we reached the coffee farm. We were up in the mountains not far from the Honduran border. There are four outposts surrounding the farm, and guards circulate twenty-four hours a day. No one goes out to pick coffee without an escort guard because the state farms are often the targets of contra attacks. But I noticed that the guards are not a special group; they are a part of the people. Many of them are just kids, quite a few are women. All have guns slung across their backs. And, to add to the open sight of arms, there was the sound of fighting in the distance.

Despite the visibility of guns and weapons, I do not feel unsafe. Though many of the militia are young men sixteen to twenty-five, they are not tense or threatening. They seem aware of their responsibility. And they are integrated into the community they defend.

I spoke to the family who lived next to our residence in Managua. The father proudly told me that at fifty-one he learned to read and write because of the Revolution. He read the newspaper to us to demonstrate his skill. He also told us about a big campaign to kill roaches. This aspect of the operation was successful, but the insecticide used to kill the roaches remained in their bodies. When the household chickens ate the roaches, they too were poisoned and died. That brought an end to that campaign.

Some of us talked to a young boy involved in the literacy program. The literacy campaign teaches reading and writing. He explained how they read about a local hero, a man who had died fighting in the Revolution. They can identify with this man because he comes from their area and he serves as an inspiration for the future and a continuity with the past. The boy also explained that, having reached a fourth grade

Nicaraguan militiawoman shows U.S. brigadista how to pick coffee. Photo by Victoria Alba.

level of reading and writing, he is now teaching other young people to read and write.

This country is so young. Most of the people are under the age of thirty. Boys and girls who look about six years old are out every day picking coffee; others who look no older than twelve have guns slung across their backs. Young women, barely matured, have babies. Many of the other people seem old. They are small, wrinkled, worn, shrunken by a hard life. It occurs to me that many people in their twenties and thirties died in the years of struggle. Also, because of hard work and hard living conditions, the people here age quickly.

One little girl at our coffee farm wanted to know if I was here without my mother. When she found out I was, she wanted to know where my mother was and how old I was. She could not believe I was twenty-one; she said women don't look as I do at twenty-one. Also women often live with their mothers until they get married and, if for any reason they part from their husbands, they go back to live with their mothers. Francisca is eleven. She stays on the farm at harvest time either picking coffee or, this season, caring for her twenty-year-old sister's baby. Otherwise she lives with her mother and siblings just outside the farm.

Francisca asked what it was like in the United States. She wanted to know about the war there. When Corinne told her that we did not have a war like in Nicaragua her eyes got large. "You mean there is no war in your country?" she asked. Corinne tried to explain that the United States made its wars in other countries, like Nicaragua. To which Francisca replied, "People just live their lives? They don't fight?" This is the reality of an eleven-year-old peasant girl.

Judith Anne Singer

In December 1983, I went to Nicaragua to pick coffee. After working two days, I was thrown off a horse while out with some Sandinista soldiers on Christmas day. I sustained seven broken ribs, a collapsed lung, a broken collar bone, and a dislocated shoulder. I was a mess and in shock.

The soldiers immediately looked for transportation to get me to the nearest hospital, which was forty miles away. This of course was a problem due to the fuel shortage caused by the bombing of Corinto in October. Meanwhile I was taken to a community shelter where I was seen by a nurse, given a pain injection, and then examined by a doctor from the nearby army barracks.

After what was easily an hour or two, a car and ambulance appeared to take me to the hospital. Both came so I could have my choice: I chose the car because I could not lie down. Two of the soldiers, a government representative, and a personal friend went with me to the hospital in Matagalpa.

When we arrived there, one of the soldiers quickly ran to inform the doctors about my condition. An x-ray was taken, and a Nicaraguan doctor who spoke a little English kept telling me everything that was going on and that I would be okay. At this point they repaired my lung, gave me more pain medication, and took me to my room. I shared my room with about twenty other women. The soldiers and my friend came to check on me.

I speak very little Spanish, but it didn't present a problem. I spent a week in that hospital and was never afraid or lonely. I was given two English books by the Nicaraguan doctor and a copy of the latest issue of *Time* magazine. I gave them away. This was not the time for me to read. Here was an opportunity for me to be with these people, to watch them, and love them.

I saw burn patients, maternity complications, and war injuries. I saw families staying at the hospital taking care of each other. Families there to be with their dying parents, mothers with their frightened young daughters. I saw smiling food workers, doctors who checked on me more than once a day, floor sweepers, and others who wanted to look at this injured North American. People who were visiting sick or injured relatives would help me eat, wash me, brush my hair, help me out of bed, push me in a wheelchair (I saw two in the whole hospital), take me outside, and bring me Pepsi.

On January 1, I was taken into town in my wheelchair to watch a fireworks display celebrating the Cuban Revolution. When I returned to the hospital, I went into the Cuban doctors' room and celebrated with them. They were very nice and concerned about me all the time I was with them. I

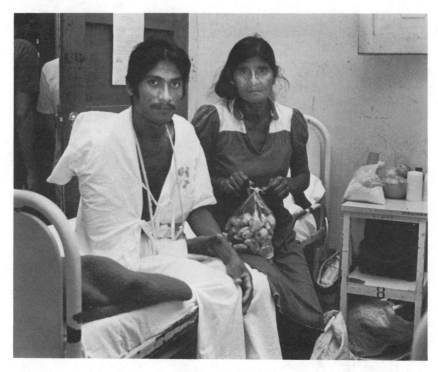

Nicaraguan soldier wounded in fighting with contras is visited by his mother in Matagalpa Hospital. Photo by Paul Tick.

became very close to a husband–wife doctor team from Cuba, and we still correspond.

Sergio Ramirez[1] was in the hospital and came over to speak with me. He told me how happy he was that North Americans were helping with the harvest. I told him it was our pleasure. He rubbed my head and smiled.

---

[1]Sergio Ramirez is a poet and writer. He was one of "The Twelve" (Los Doce), a group of well-known Nicaraguan leaders who got together in 1978 and openly supported the FSLN's armed struggle to overthrow Somoza. He was elected vice president of Nicaragua on November 4, 1984.

Gail Sangree

I decided around Thanksgiving time that I would like to go to Nicaragua to assist in the coffee, rice, and cotton harvests. I did so in order to learn more about the country that my daughter Suzie had fallen in love with when she went there for the year in 1981. I also wanted to help the economy of a nation under great stress from what I perceive as a misguided U.S. government policy. Planning for a two week trip, I worried that I wouldn't be able to adapt to the difficult living conditions, doing without tea, without my before-dinner cocktail, without the bathtub. But I decided to risk it. I worried that the young people would want to stay up late while I would be trying to sleep. The scant printed material I received beforehand stressed the need for flexibility and that we should be prepared for anything. This turned out to be good advice.

Saturday, December 31

I flew to Miami and had my first lesson in flexibility. Upon our arrival at the Aeronica center, we learned our flight had been postponed until Monday.

Monday, January 2

We held a press conference at the Miami airport and then left at 3:00 PM for Managua. There we were greeted by many friendly people and taken through customs. We delivered the medical supplies we had brought to donate, changed sixty U.S. dollars into 1,675 cordobas, and we then went to EMSEC, a conference center outside of Managua with nice accommodations. That night we learned that we were going south to work on farms by the Costa Rican border.

Tuesday, January 3

I walked on the road before breakfast. Naked children on dusty path, which mother is sweeping. We have a meeting to pool medical supplies. We are shipping out tomorrow for a boat ride on Lake Nicaragua to the Río San Juan area where we will be clearing land. We listen to a half hour talk about how we will be helping the people while working among the poisonous snakes (called ox killers) and clouds of mosquitos.

Several of us walked to the market place in the afternoon. Our picture was on the front page of the newspaper, so a lot of people knew who we were.

Wednesday, January 4

I am sitting on the roof of the boat, the Lynx, looking back at Granada, a beautiful old Spanish town. There were cows in the yard of the art museum. The Lynx arrives at San Carlos at 12:30 AM. There is much confusion for an hour until we are escorted up a dusty flight of steps to a dingy school where there are little straw mattresses for us on the floor. School is on vacation for January.

Thursday, January 5

Awoke at 6:30 AM and found there was running water to wash with in the schoolyard and a real bathroom down the hill. The streets are rutted mud. The houses are of cement or wood, with corrugated tin roofs. Nothing is pretty, but it is a happy functioning community with lots of public play places, a park for the children, a small stadium, a corner with benches and umbrellas. The laundromat is a roofed area of big stones at the lake's edge where washing occupies a large portion of the women's time. There are no beggars here, and nobody is starving.

We were told that we would be paid the minimum wage for our labors. Everyone protested loudly that we did not want to be paid. But the Nicaraguans want to keep track of the costs of production. We are free to donate the money we earn as we wish.

We are divided into three groups, the largest of which will remain at San Carlos. One group of twenty-five will harvest rice, and another group of thirty-three will work at a cattle ranch called Morrillo on Lake Nicaragua, a former Somoza plantation. Somoza owned 35 percent of the land in Nicaragua. We board boats again, spend a night in another school at San Miguelito and are delivered the next day to Morrillo. This place is now a large state farm with 280 people. Somoza's old cottage is an attractive log cabin-style hacienda with a red stone floor and bedrooms off the living area. A huge porch surrounds the house, the only building in Morrillo with flush toilets. Now an agricultural school, this is to be our home. After rice and beans, we go exploring. The cattle are Brahmins. They stroll about accompanied by white birds who eat the parasites off their backs. I went swimming in the lake, and it felt good, though there are little things that bite you as you stand in the water. The women tell us they are sardines and not dangerous.

Friday, January 6

Last night we had an ugly confrontation with some drunk Germans. They had a couple of bottles of rum and wanted to sing and laugh outside our door. Several of our group went out and begged them to be quiet. They called us a "new example of imperialism." They were rude, loud, and refused to leave. Finally, they said their feelings were hurt because such a fuss was being made over the North Americans when they had been here working hard for three weeks.

Our first day of work! I worked in the vegetable garden this morning with Ellen, a stout earnest Quaker woman in her sixties from Albany, and two other young women. We watered and weeded thousands of tomato plants using hands, hoes, machetes. As we worked, there was an assortment of children with us, talking and helping, chasing out the pigs who could squeeze under the barbed wire. Children are not excluded from anything here: they are constantly with adults and assume without hesitation tasks that the adults are performing.

The garden is roughly an acre in size, lovely black topsoil with few stones. A well at the foot of the garden provides water for the plants: soybeans, radishes, melons, peppers. Papaya and banana trees line the periphery with huge fruit.

Other groups were digging trenches for protection from bombs, which everyone fears, herding cattle onto boats for San Miguelito, and loading rocks onto the back of a tractor to fill holes in the road. This group killed a rattler and a coral snake the first morning.

After morning work, we visited the health center and learned that this region had no health services at all three years ago. Now there is a nurse in attendance every day and a doctor who comes once a week. They have an active program of vaccinations for the children and take preventive measures to reduce respiratory diseases and diarrhea.

This afternoon I went to the rock piles. We filled the flatbed behind the tractor, then drove to a place in the road where a mudhole needed to be filled. It's nice to see the countryside as we ride, but the work is dangerous because of spiders as big as your fist and the coral snakes, two more of which were killed by the tractor driver. These snakes are responsible for deaths among the cattle. If killed by a coral snake, the meat is poisoned and cannot be used.

At a meeting after dinner, we discussed the problem of our relationship with the children. Some felt that there were problems with our gift giving (chocolates, yo yo's, pens, and buttons) and that the children's parents would have a hard time with the kids after we were gone. It was decided that in the future we would give gifts anonymously in a bunch to the adults and let them handle the distribution.

Sunday, January 8

This afternoon we took a boat trip to San José. We went down past Solentiname to the San José River, which we then followed to a farm that had only recently become part of the state farm system. In November, it was taken over by the government from a landowner who was not cooperating with the goals set forth by the agricultural committee. He spent most of his time in the United States, while his cattle starved. He will be paid for the stock and movable items like tractors, but not for the land.

Monday, January 9

A few women of the community come to visit in the evening. Shy and dressed up, they introduce themselves. Elena is thirty, expects her eighth child, has no man permanently in the household. She takes in laundry, sells things, and kills pigs to eke out a living. She hopes that in the future real jobs will become available for women because life has always been hard for her. She looks for a better life for her children rather than herself. She points out that progress has been made since the triumph. Now there is a health center and educational opportunities that did not exist a few years ago. Some of the young girls talk about their schooling. They are in fifth and sixth grades (about thirteen and fourteen years old), spend half a day in school, the other half staffing the preschool. Now there are four teachers for the seventy students at Morrillo. There used to be only one.

They have heard about the women's movement on TV, but it has not reached here yet. To encourage stability, the government has passed a law that men must be responsible for their families. Speaking of TV, Ann Peters watched a station from Costa Rica this evening. She saw an ad for a men's deodorant, which promised to make the girls turn their heads and fall in love. It is called "Green Beret."

Wednesday, January 11

Today we worked in the garden morning and afternoon, uncovering a lot of tomato plants that had been completely engulfed by weeds. After lunch a young woman in her fourth year of medical school spoke to us about medical care before and after the triumph. The medical school has grown from 90 students to 550. Tuition is free. It is aided by medical brigades from Bulgaria, Cuba, the Soviet Union, and the United States. Some students are sent abroad for special study, and many foreign doctors come here to assist in training. She is currently on her vacation, but she is spending it visiting all the health centers in this area. "Although I am not a doctor, I've had enough training to know how to care for a child with parasites or with diarrhea," she says.

This evening there was a spirited discussion about Bob, who has mechanical skills and has been working for two days in San Miguelito fixing engines. He has been asked to stay on and intends to leave the group in order to continue the work. "If one of you can give me a bottle of Maalox, that's all I ask," he says. But people are worried that Bob should not take it upon himself to leave, something we have been specifically told not to do. When it came to a vote, it was decided that he should delay until it is cleared with our group leader who is in San Carlos.

Thursday, January 12

Everyone here thinks they have lost weight. We joke about what a wonderful idea it would be to promote a vacation in sunny Nicaragua with a guaranteed weight loss of ten pounds per week.

More of our group are sick. It looks like no one will escape.

Friday, January 13

Worked digging the trench by the health center for a couple of hours this morning. Nine of us plus the usual assortment of children. It is big enough for fifteen people, and is about four feet deep now. After a while, neighborhood women bring us lemonade.

Nicaraguans and North American brigadistas in the cotton fields. Photo by Victor Sanchez.

After lunch we are having a meeting deciding where to donate our salaries when word arrives that the boat leaves for San Carlos in one hour. Pandemonium. We pack the stuff we don't intend to give away, donate the clothes, medicines, and other things to the community leaders, say a hurried and totally inadequate good-bye, and pile onto the boat.

Barbara Leon

Punta Ñata is named for its shape, a small snub-nose of a peninsula protruding off Nicaragua's Pacific coast on the southern part of the Gulf of Fonseca. Looking across the water, one can see the mountains of El Salvador and Honduras, Nicaragua's hostile neighbors to the north. The peaceful landscape of green and white cottonfields set against a backdrop of blue sky and volcanoes belies the bloody conflict going on over control of the land.

At night the only sight visible on the horizon is a constellation of bright lights in Honduras. These lights, we soon learned, are those of the United States-Honduran-contra military base in San Lorenzo. It was less than two weeks before our arrival that this base was used to launch an attack on the small Nicaraguan port of Potosi, about twelve miles from Punta Ñata. The attack by aircraft and gunboats lasted for six straight days in early January, killing a twenty-five-year-old militia member, wounding six civilians, and destroying several buildings and houses. The entire population of 1,200 campesinos, cattle farmers, and fishermen was evacuated to another town, where they were still living.

> *Salvador is the crew leader assigned to oversee the North American production brigade. He moves quickly between the rows, deftly picking balls of cotton and stuffing them into our bags to make them a little heavier. He is unable to suppress an amused smile at the paltry pickings some of us bring to the weighing station.*
>
> *During a work break, Salvador talks to us about the importance of raising production. Since the Revolution, he says, the workers have a direct stake in increasing productivity because they know that more cotton means more food, more medicines, improved housing. And they are glad when they see production money go into the purchase of new farming equipment, he says, because that in turn means even greater production that will be used to benefit the workers.*
>
> *When we ask Salvador how life has changed since the Revolution, he immediately begins to talk about the literacy classes. Most of them are held in the peasants' own houses, with the people who have learned basic reading and writing acting as "maestros populares"—popular teachers—for those just below them on the educational scale.*
>
> *Salvador talks about how important it is for Nicaraguan workers to learn to read, in order to be able to learn what is going on in the world. For instance, Nicaraguan campesinos cannot understand their own situation if they do not understand the history and politics of the United States, he says. And if they do not understand their own situation they can do nothing to change it.*

By day the Gulf of Fonseca appears still and empty, hardly what one would expect at the site depicted by the United States government as a major supply route for armaments allegedly sent from Nicaragua to the Salvadoran revolutionaries. The only activity visible on the gulf is the occasional appearance of a United States frigate patrolling the coast. "La frigata," as the villagers call it, is a constant presence in Punta Ñata; until our arrival, it was the only North American presence. "It is there because the United States wants to invade our country," a small child explained.

Punta Ñata is the largest farm in the region, with 500 to 700 year-round residents, a figure that doubles at the height of the cotton harvest. Until its nationalization last May, Punta Ñata belonged to a corporation whose principal figure was Alfonso Robelo, a contra leader associated with former Sandinista Eden Pastora. Robelo is depicted in the Western press as a liberal, even a socialist, who fought against Somoza and tried to work with the Sandinistas as a member of the newly-formed revolutionary government. According to this view, Robelo broke with the revolution when he saw it had been "betrayed."

But the farmworkers of Punta Ñata tell a different story. Robelo broke with the Sandinistas, they say, when he saw that the revolution would be more than a change in faces at the top. Specifically, Robelo broke with the Sandinistas when the government insisted he obey the new laws improving conditions for agricultural workers, the workers explained.

According to Juan Francisco Río, production chief at Punta Ñata and a former leader of the farmworkers union, Robelo's resistance to change led to work stoppages in 1980. The work stoppages made a difference, he said. New housing was built, a second row of outhouses and showers were added, wages were raised to the government-decreed minimum, and a doctor was assigned to the farm. Robelo resigned from the government. Within two years he had left the country and taken up arms against the revolution.

Aaron introduced himself to us as we swam in the ocean. Now seventeen years old and a militante in the Sandinista youth, he was on vacation visiting a relative in a nearby village. Aaron first became involved in the struggle when he was an eleven-year-old street vendor selling bread in the center of Chinandega, he told us. He made the mistake of getting too close to National Guard headquarters in the town and was arrested on suspicion of being a spy. At the time of his arrest, Aaron said, he knew nothing about the guerrillas. Nevertheless, he was tortured for several hours and the lives of his family threatened before a delegation of street peddlers were able to convince the police they had made a mistake. After his release, Aaron decided to find out who these guerrillas were who were fighting the Guard. Within a short time, he had gone underground and joined the armed struggle.

To North Americans, the poverty at Punta Ñata is still overwhelming. The hot, dry climate in this region of Nicaragua is essential for proper development of the cotton crop, but for the inhabitants of Punta Ñata it means that everything is perpetually covered with a film of dust. The row housing is small and dark. Children run around barefoot in the dirt, their feet picking up parasites that will later cause serious illness. The water supply is contaminated by bacteria and residues of the pesticides that are only now coming under government control. At mid-afternoon, the water supply is usually exhausted, and the villagers must wait for the tank truck to arrive with a new supply.

Still, the residents tell us, things are much better than before the Revolution. Now there is enough food to eat, with occasional meat, fruits, and vegetables to supplement the rice, beans, and tortillas that are served three times a day. Polio has been wiped out and malaria reduced to a few cases per year in the region. Not only the children, but even the adults, have learned to read and write. But there is still much more to be done, they say, and much more that could be done if the resources of the country were not diverted to fighting off the contra gains.

The day begins at Punta Ñata at 3:30 AM. Continual, loud blasts from the horn of a truck awaken the population. Soon fires are going in the houses of the year-round families and the communal kitchens that feed the migrant workers. A rhythmic slapping emanates from all corners of the farm, the sound of women preparing the coarse, thick tortillas that are a staple of life here.

For the North American brigadistas, the morning starts a little later. We get up at 5 AM, making our way to the outhouses and the large concrete cistern where we can scoop out enough water to wash our hands and faces. Nearby in the darkness some of the village women are already washing clothes with thick bars of laundry soap and buckets of water from the cistern. They rub the clothing back and

> On the beach, a large circle had formed. A woman soldier had agreed to talk with the brigadistas, to tell of her experiences in the old and the new Nicaragua. She was a little apprehensive—we were asked not to write down her name—and puzzled as to why this group of North Americans wanted to hear her story and her opinions. But she relaxed when one of our group explained our interest in learning about Nicaragua from firsthand experience so as to be able to spread this knowledge to our own people.
>
> We asked her whether the position of women in Nicaragua had changed since the Revolution and received a mixed response. She was armed and doing her share to defend against contra attack, but she had also come to the beach that day to cook for the male soldiers, one of the functions of the female army units. The Revolution has made many changes for women, she said, but special problems remain.
>
> The most important thing the Revolution did for Nicaraguan women, she said, was free them to leave their homes and do political work. Once they were outside, the old marital patterns could not continue unchanged. They were also able to organize into women's associations to deal with their problems as women.
>
> Women still encounter resistance from their husbands, she said, but the degree varies with the general political consciousness of the man. The more he understands the general needs of Nicaragua, the more sympathetic he usually is to the particular needs of Nicaraguan women. Meanwhile, the Revolution has made it legitimate for women to fight, to work in jobs formerly reserved for men, and to participate in the political process, she said. From that, changes in the personal relationships between men and women would follow.

forth on the ribbed, concrete washing boards to remove the thick dust, then hang the clothes on improvised clotheslines made of barbed wire. Some of the women must move quickly, for they must be in the fields at dawn.

At the kitchen, a breakfast line is forming. The North Americans have been instructed to bring mess kits and utensils, since we are not used to eating our food out of tortillas. Along with our food, we are served sweetened, instant coffee. Nicaragua is renowned for its coffee crop, but the needs of the economy dictate that the best beans be grown for export, a cash crop that provides the foreign

Making tortillas. Photo by Paul Tick.

exchange needed to rebuild the country after the devastation of the civil war. Today, that foreign exchange is also needed to finance the defense effort against the contras, to replace the fuel oil destroyed by contra attacks, and to buy the medicines in scarce supply due to the United States economic boycott.

As the sun rises we are in the fields. It is impossible to pick cotton in the midday heat of Nicaragua, so harvesting must be done in the cooler hours of early morning and late afternoon. The brigadistas follow the same picking schedule as the Nicaraguan workers: 6–10 AM, then a break of several hours, with a return to the fields from about 3–5 PM. The six-hour day is an innovation of the Sandinistas; in the past, workers stayed in the fields for eight hours a day. The two hours of labor saved are used for adult literacy classes in the evening.

The picking does not seem difficult at first, a simple matter of reaching inside the opened pods and removing in one piece the attached ball of cotton. It soon becomes evident, however, that the cotton bags attached to our waists are not filling at the same rate as those of the Nicaraguans supervising us, and the work seems much more difficult as the heat of the day increases.

Although there is a daily minimum wage, picking is still paid at piece rates, we learn. As we line up at the weighing station at the end of the first day we find we would barely survive if we had to depend on the proceeds of our own picking.

Our first view of Punta Ñata had been one of noise, dust, and disorganization. As we lived and worked with the Nicaraguan people, we realized just how misleading that first impression had been and how much energy and efficiency went into keeping this farm running.

Margaret Lobenstine

"Many Americans know very little about Nicaragua," I said. "North Americans," she corrected me gently. Slowly my consciousness grew: Americans live throughout two continents. What right do we, as citizens of the United States, just one country among many in the Western hemisphere, have to take that term as our own private property?

Pictures

Looking out the window from a bus in Managua to see an ox cart and a Mercedes waiting side by side at the red light. Realizing that as long as the owners of either contribute to production, they are crucial to Nicaragua.

Each morning, after awakening around 5, I would walk through the predawn darkness to the latrines, my path lit by the cooking fires of the women already preparing breakfast for their families. A long day later, passing the same way again, I would see those same women, still up, with an iron in their hand. Amid the dust and the dirt and the shortages of water, their pride fights back with an iron.

Standing by the cotton weighing truck, one can see the lush green hills of El Salvador and Honduras across the sparkling blue waters of the Gulf of Fonseca. I want to imagine a peaceful tropical paradise, but the three U.S. frigates sit below us, hulking grey ships of death, reminders.

Six o'clock in the morning. Time to leave for the cotton fields. Inevitably some among us are still rushing around looking for our cotton sack rope, our canteen, our hat, remembering to take our antimalaria pill, finishing breakfast. All to the background of the Sandinista Juventud, the Nicaraguan student brigades, who are stepping out promptly, proudly, chanting "Sandino Vive!" in such a spirited, disciplined way.

It's dark. Our bus is packed to the brim with half of our brigade, more than sixty of us, and all our backpacks, sleeping bags, suitcases. The dirt road is thick with dust, winding, gutted, steep. So treacherous in fact that a jeep has been sent out to guide the bus driver. We're tired from the long ride out from Managua, eager to arrive at the cotton farm that will be our home. When the tire goes, we groan. When we realize the spare is stored *behind* all our baggage, we wonder how long we'll be stuck. But then the Nicaraguans move us quickly, smoothly, into such a coordinated action that the tire is changed, the luggage reloaded, and all of us are back on board and rolling in less than twenty minutes. So that's what working collectively does!

Memories

There she sat. Her gun across her lap, held gently by gnarled brown fingers. Her face crinkled, her eyes set deep. At first she was puzzled why the Norteamericanos would find her of interest, but she was more than willing to try answering our questions. Yes, she's a member of the militia. Yes, she fought in the Revolution. Yes, she supports the Sandinistas. Why? Her answer is quietly told: before the Revolution "all she was" was a washerwoman. A washerwoman working at home, surrounded by her kids. Never allowed to go anywhere but mass and market, just washing. But the Sandinistas saw past that, saw her potential as a human being. They respected her enough to trust her, with secrets, weapons. She became one of their night time couriers. The National Guard got suspicious. Several times they even came to her house. But each time they saw no more than what Somoza and his class had always seen—"only a washerwoman." They went away convinced she could not be relevant. I can see why today she stands guard with, attends classes with, and will certainly vote with the Sandinistas; they not only ended Somoza's power, they also recognized hers.

I happened to look out over the crowded meeting in front of me. There at the back of the room, all alone, stood a young man, trying to phone. I knew immediately who he must be, the fellow from the brigade working in the south of Nicaragua whose mother had died unexpectedly. I went over to be with him. "They sent a plane for me," he said. "They brought me up here by plane!" In fuel-desperate Nicaragua, where U.S.-supplied bombs had attacked a major oil storage area just a few months earlier, a *plane* had been sent south to help facilitate this man's sad return home. I was struck by the love implicit in such an action. And I thought of the generosity with which we had been fed and sheltered since our arrival in Managua. Then suddenly, for some reason, I flashed on World War II. When Germany and Japan were our country's enemies, we were supposed to hate *all* Germans, all "Japs." No distinction was made between the emperor of Japan and the small children with Japanese heritage we interned in concentration camps on our west coast. Yet despite the fact that U.S. marines basically occupied Nicaragua from 1912 to 1933, that the U.S. established the dictatorship of the Somoza family and trained its hated National Guard, that today the U.S. government is openly supporting contra attacks on the sovereign state of Nicaragua and talks explicitly about "not being able to live with" the Sandinista government, the Nicaraguan people still lovingly distinguish between the people of our country and its government. They wanted our baseball cards, they wanted to see pictures of our families, and they used up precious fuel to send a plane for one of us whose mother had died.

I just couldn't see how he did it. This twenty-three-year-old FSLN soldier with his open smile, obvious sense of humor, and seemingly inexhaustible enthusiasm. "Keep asking me questions! You need to know whatever you want to know so you can share with your people when you go home! I'm not tired." He had repeated this over and over during the hot Saturday afternoon, despite the fact that he'd worked all Friday and been up all Friday night on watch duty. So after the discussion was over, I asked him my personal question. "How do you handle it when you get demoralized? I feel so impotent sometimes in the U.S., get so discouraged, and you are up against such a *powerful* enemy." He thought for a moment as the sun set behind him. His answer has remained with me: "I don't think I'll ever have that sense you are talking about. Because I know I can die for our future. My body will be in the earth before we lose Nicaragua." He can make a difference.

Understandings

Yes I know the U.S. government has been attacking the Sandinista government with economic sanctions as well as with guns. That vague generality takes on shape and substance when sodas are drunk from baggies (a bottle shortage), a young father can't photograph his eight-month-old daughter (there's no film), when the nine-year-old screams out all night from the pain of rheumatoid arthritis (the medicine and pain killers she needs are not available), when crop dusting planes inadvertently dust living areas because their nozzles are too old to close completely (the U.S. has cut off the means to get replacements). When trucks don't work, crops don't get harvested; when there's a paper shortage, the national women's organization can't leaflet rural women with information they need. When phone lines are down or the only "phone service" is an old shortwave radio, two groups waste precious resources preparing separate lunches for the same 130 brigadistas. The CIA would like to blame such losses on the "inefficient Sandinistas"—but it is U.S. policy that brings that child her screams. As long as the U.S. tightens the economic noose around Nicaragua, it wields a weapon as deadly as a gun. We must oppose both!

Editor's Note

On February 2, 1984, members of the Maura Clarke Brigade were on their way to two small farms in the northwest corner of Nicaragua: Punta Ñata and Apascalí. They heard what sounded like fireworks and saw what looked like lightning. Returning from their first day of work in the cotton fields, the brigadistas learned that they had observed two bombing raids. One attack killed four and injured eleven members of the Nicaraguan people's militia; the other destroyed a radio communications center.

Returning home two weeks later, the brigadistas protested the air attacks, which the Nicaraguans blamed on the CIA. In the spring days of 1984, our government still maintained the fiction of covert war and denied responsibility.

In late April, Honduras-based contras told two visiting U.S. congressmen, Bill Alexander and Wyche Fowler, Jr., that the bombing raids had been carried out by a non-Nicaraguan, CIA-led, Latin American commando unit. The CIA was not only financing the contras, but using them as cover for other mercenaries.

When the congressmen's findings were reported in the U.S. press (*The Fresno Bee*, May 3, 1984), one Maura Clarke brigadista from Fresno, California, Doug Hammerstrom, wrote:

> The morning headline reads "U.S. Role in Nicaraguan Air Strike." The headline refers to bombings of a radio transmitter and a military camp on February 2, 1984. Members of the Maura Clarke brigade witnessed this bombing as we made our way north to pick cotton.
>
> The steam built in me as I recalled my outrage at U.S. actions in Central America and how that incident personalized and made real the incidents before about which I had only read. My outrage grew as I thought of the chilly reception and biting challenges I have received

to my public assertions that those raids were carried out by the CIA. So many people are resistant to seeing the truth of the horror of U.S. involvement in Central America.

Suzanne Sangree

The National Network people called me just as the brigade was leaving and asked me to be an assistant leader. I had lived in Nicaragua for a year, helping to found Casa Nicaragüense de Español, a Spanish language school. I was feeling very burned out, so I asked them what it would entail. They said that the job would be to watch out for problems and that everything was organized down there. So I said I would do it.

I went down a week early to visit friends. When I met up with the brigade, I found my job description had become that of coleader and that nothing was organized. We had 170 people that were about to leave to go up into what turned out to be a military zone. This was on the Gulf of Fonseca in the northern department of Chinandega. There had been no contra activity in months, but, as we were driving up there, there was a bombing of a communications center about thirty kilometers from the farm where we stayed.

We took all day to get there. First in buses in Chinandega, then in trucks, over these winding up- and downhill roads. On the way, some people in the trucks saw the explosions. We arrived after dark to a dinner and a rousing welcome. We were taken to the bunks, which were stacked three floors high. We decided only to use the ones up to the second floor. It was hard to get up there.

The first night I was given a briefing by the Nicaraguan leadership. They told us we would need tighter security than planned because there had been some recent contra activity. We had to have a 9:00 PM curfew with all lights out. No one was allowed to sleep outside of the bunkhouse. Movement outside after dark was to be minimized.

Sometime between two and three in the morning I heard all of a sudden loud motor sounds. Then I heard Nicaraguans running outside. I thought, "Oh my god, there's an attack going on." So I forgot that I was twelve feet high and swung over the edge. I dropped down and smashed my toe on the dirt floor. I limped barefoot out of the bunkhouse and asked someone, "What's going on?" And they said, "It's the bus to Chinandega!"

My toe was throbbing and full of dirt, but we had made no arrangement for the medical responsables to be on call that night. So I sat on my bunk until sunrise.

The toe became infected right away, and the doctors told me to stay out of the fields. It was good because I was able to get to know the Nicaraguans and set up meetings with them for the brigade. One man, Lorenzo, had been on the farm since he was four. Now he was fifty-one. He badly injured his hand in a tractor accident while I was there. He came walking into the central living area with his hand bandaged and bloody. I told him I would ask one of our doctors to look at his hand, but he wasn't interested. He had never had any medical care in his life.

I insisted, however, and Andrew, who is a "barefoot" doctor in the Appalachian mountains of West Virginia, came. He had his kit, with everything he would need to stitch Lorenzo up. Two medical students from León had been stationed on the hacienda as their social service, and they wanted to learn how to stitch up and take care of such an injury. Poor Lorenzo—between my squeamishness, Andrew's lack of Spanish, and the medical students' questions, it took a while to fix him up.

Sox Sperry

Dear Family and Friends:

After deep introspection, I decided to go to Nicaragua to participate in the harvest in response to the Nicaraguan government's request for assistance from North American friends. This action struck me as an active and nonviolent way to oppose the Reagan government's warmaking in the region, to support the Nicaraguan people's right to determine their own future, and to gain first-hand knowledge of the situation in Nicaragua.

This was not an easy decision for me. I was aware of the implicit danger of walking into a war zone at a time when the air was thick with rumors of imminent invasion. I had no desire to become another war casualty. What lifted me beyond my fear was the hope that my going to Nicaragua, along with those other U.S. citizens who were joining the harvest, would be a step toward peace and away from war. We followed our own definition of deterrence in the hope that, by observing and then speaking the truth as we saw it, we would help to deter the violence we witnessed.

I went to Nicaragua with an awareness of the risks, while at the same time not wanting to over-dramatize the act. As North Americans, we were likely to be far safer than most Nicaraguans in their own country. The Nicaraguan government has stated that volunteer work brigades will not be sent into areas where their safety cannot be assured.

Obviously no place in Nicaragua is completely "secured" against contra attack or against a U.S. decision to invade. It seems clear to me that in taking the risk of going to Nicaragua we became hostages of our own country's violence and not that of some "enemy" people.

I composed this poem during my stay in Punta Ñata, a hacienda in the northwest corner of Nicaragua on the Gulf of Fonseca. In the evenings after picking, we'd walk down to the cliff overlooking the sea. There we'd sit and watch the sun cast the final brilliance of its day into the waters of the Pacific and the clouds above. A moment of peace, shared among North American and Nicaraguan brigadistas. Later in the evening, we would see the lights of the U.S. warships. This poem reflects the spirit of hundreds of returning brigadistas who are now giving our hands to the harvest of peace in the communities to which we have returned.

El Fuego de Punta Ñata

dedicated to:
Reynaldo Sequeira
Felix Somarriba

I   Punta Ñata, Nicaragua
     February 3, 1984

5AM
the ember glow of breakfast fires
the soft parade to the latrine
the roosters' raucous chant
signal a rising
into the precious cool of predawn

standing, my gaze falls to the horizon
shark tooth lights puncture the night
the US frigata and its piranha boat fleet
burn crosses on the sea
betraying the pacific waters
on which they trespass

6AM
cottonfields rise white and drifting
through the solid sky of morning
in the background, Volcán Cosiqüina
grandmother to these fields of dust and cotton
her fire long since spent
at peace now with her children beneath

from the clear sky
beyond the silent mountain
thunder rolls, the earth trembles
eyes and ears question the dawn
no answers forthcoming

7PM
night surrounds the ancient Ceiba tree
centerpiece of the village
overseer of these gentle paths
tortillas on the fire
shadows dance to a Latin beat
children's laughter rolling with their hoops

into this soft collaboration of the senses
an urgent call—"Barricada! Barricada!"
the evening paper arrives
dos centavos into a tiny palm
the headlines recall the thunder of the morning
"Agresiones deterioran perspectivas de paz"
"Attacks damage prospect for peace"
Manzanilla, Chinandega

at 6AM on the morning of February 3
(I face the sun with beans and rice)
four Push and Pull fighter-bombers
army-green, unmarked
flying from Honduras
violate Nicaraguan airspace
they bomb a unit of the EPS
(beyond this mountain)
leaving seven Nicaraguans wounded
several fuel deposits destroyed

the previous evening's target
(we thought we saw fireworks in the distance)
a radio installation of the
Ministry of Agricultural Development and Agrarian Reform
four Nicaraguans dead, four more wounded

my paycheck delivers
the Internal Revenue Service
the Federal Treasury
the Central Intelligence Agency
the Honduran military
the blood of fifteen Nicaraguan citizens

II   December 1983–February 1984

seven hundred North Americans cross the border
into Nicaragua Libre
we offer
our hands to the harvest
and eyes and ears to understanding
our hearts to peace

we labor
in the cottonfields and coffee plantations of the north
in the jungles of the south

we harvest fiber for an international cloth
spinning the stories which bring us to this passage
weaving new patterns to carry us home
this work, the fabric of our journey

with the Nicaraguans we place our bodies
between sun and soil, entre sol y tierra
between the deathships and the shore
De la Frontera No Pasaran!

for us the moment passes quickly
for the Nicaraguans
this danger does not end
with a flight back home
for the Nicaraguans
this is home

III   El Fuego de Punta Ñata

the searing sun, dust on the wind
cotton in the fields, rice and beans in the pot
mother earth to 2½ million people
born in fire

volcanic fire
lava bursting into air, into flames, into earth
furnace of the midday sun
bending all living things to its demands
flames of revolution
burning in the chants of the Juventud
melting in the dance of the children
forging a determination to defend this land
at all costs
Patria Libre o Morir!

these fires
earth, sun, spirit
home fires, flames of life

the cold lights of the warships before dawn
the metal flash of bullets
flesh cut from bone
screams torn from slumber
hold none of nature's fire

reflecting false heat, fractured light
cold flames wither
outside the circle of life
death frozen in their shadow

what demands shall we make
of these war merchants
with their fluorescent, microwave
pretense of holy crusade?

what light can we throw
to illuminate their lies?

what heat can we generate
to cleanse the wounds they make?

Here, in Nicaragua Libre
I find the source
flames of resistance
kindled with courage
lit with dialogue
fanned with determination
tended with love

in this light
we may yet find our return

Brigadista Stuart Selmon picking cotton at Punta Ñata. Photo by Victor Sanchez.

to those home fires
smouldering still
in our north land

Shana Saper

There was a serious shortage of water in Apascalí, and what there was was bad to drink. Bad because sewage and pesticide run-off had contaminated the wells, and malfunctioning pumps just compounded the problem. Despite the best efforts of the village clinic, diarrhea and dehydration plagued the local people as well as us. Adults manage to live with bacterial parasites and infections, but as we learned, children aren't so lucky.

A baby girl, eight months old, died today of septic infection and malnutrition. The child's mother, having discovered she was pregnant again, had stopped breast-feeding her for fear of harming the baby inside. Instead, the mother put her so-far healthy infant on an adult's diet of beans, rice, and bad water. Soon, the baby began running a high fever and showing signs of severe dehydration; before two days, she was dead.

Reaction to the death was universal and public. The little body lay outdoors on a white cloth-draped table for twenty-four hours. Mourners came to sit vigil while the young mother, swelling with new life, looked on, numbed and tired. People offered their sympathies, expressing comfort and hope for the child to come. But to each other, they spoke of malfunctioning pumps: if the pumps were more powerful, if we could get parts to fix the machinery, then babies wouldn't die.

As the baby's body was being laid in its grave, a crew back in the village was busy digging another hole in the ground. This one big enough to shelter live people from bombs. The war was on their doorstep. But as everyone knew, the war kills not with bombs and bullets alone.

Becky Thorne

On September 5, 1984, two North American work teams—the Martin Luther King and Maura Clarke brigades—delivered over 5,500 dollars worth of material aid to the Nicaraguan cotton plantations of Punta Ñata and Apascalí: two ten horsepower pumps and parts to rebuild one John Deere tractor. The donation was the result of diverse fundraising activities carried out by some 280 brigade members throughout the U.S. The delivery was made by fundraising directors Dave Brown and myself.

Editor's Note

Becky and Dave toured five potential well sites with a water engineer and reported that the pumps could not have arrived at a more appropriate time; farm administrators stated that there had been serious water problems for the past three months. Lorenzo Aleman, Secretary of the Association of Field Workers at Apascalí, sent this message to all brigadistas and friends involved with the project:

> We know that through love and sacrifice, these people have returned here a second time to show their moral and material support of the society we are constructing. When we see people like this, we know they are not a part of Reagan. Sure, they are North Americans. But what we have here in front of us right now—and all over North America—are our brothers.

Joyce Stoller

The papers in the U.S. are spiked with the news that Nicaragua is a military threat not just to its neighbors, but to the United States as well. This may come as something of a surprise to Nicaragua, which has no air force and only two commercial airplanes that fly out of the country. One flies to Mexico City every day. The other to Miami.[1] It took three days to shuttle the 152 North Americans on our brigade from Miami to Managua.

Once all three planeloads of us arrived in Managua, the first thing we had to do was give ourselves a name. We chose Maura Clarke, the North American nun who had lived for many years in Managua before she and three other church women were raped and assassinated by security forces in El Salvador.

On our way out of Managua, we stopped at the U.S. embassy to protest the misuse of our tax dollars. United States Ambassador Anthony Quainton refused to meet with us, calling us "antisocial elements." Our protest was widely reported in Nicaragua, and, in a baseball game we later had with the Nicaraguans at the cotton farm, they dubbed us the "antisocials" versus the "socialists."

On the final leg of our trip to Apascalí in the department of Chinandega, we had to ride standing up in cattle cars because buses could no longer navigate the rock-strewn roads. Cotton country is beautiful in Nicaragua. Red earth, white fields, smoking volcanoes in the distance. One moun-

---

[1]All Aeronica flights to the United States were banned by President Reagan on May 7, 1985, when he imposed an economic embargo on all commercial trade with Nicaragua.

tain, Volcán Cosigüina, was especially beautiful as it arched blue and gold into the clouds.

Apascalí is located on the peninsula that juts into the Gulf of Fonseca, not far from Honduras. Besides farmworkers, the town is home to Honduran and Nicaraguan refugees, some of the 56,000 who have fled from border areas.

The state farm used to have thirty John Deere tractors, but because of the U.S.-imposed trade embargo, they can't get replacement parts, and now there are only sixteen tractors that work. There were no paved roads, no electricity in the huts, no sewage system, no running water. What water there was was stored in open pesticide barrels, and kids drank freely from these.

After an attack on a neighboring town, we offered to go there and help rebuild. Because of logistical problems, due in part to the fact that the communications tower had been bombed, we were asked to help by digging a bomb shelter where we were. Apascalí already had two bomb shelters. We dug a third.

Eugene Novogrodsky

Baseball Brings Together All Segments of Society

There I was in Nicaragua, a North American brigadista picking cotton, when baseball kept appearing. That's how my life has usually been—no matter how grim things are going, there's been baseball, that game of games.

Two kids stood in a dusty street in Chinandega, an agricultural and business city, and played catch. The ball was worn down to its core and was hard to handle. But it also made curves easier to throw.

Three kids came to see the brigadistas, who were standing at the tip of Nicaragua's northwest peninsula. The brigadistas discussed the spectacular geography—and the region's fame (thanks to military matters). But the kids only wanted to play ball. One, nicknamed "Señor Curva" (Mr. Curve Ball) had a marvelous sinker-hook—those worn balls. He was twelve. His two pals tried to emulate the pitch. They were okay, but hardly up to Señor Curva's class.

Six brigadistas went to an old stadium in downtown Managua to see Managua play León in the national semis.

The game began at 10:00 AM. Managua, with a rally, won 5–2. About 10,000 fans stood the whole game and constantly talked about the plays. Most rooted for Managua. The stadium was full, although the game was televised. Baseball minus scoreboards and with rapt fans is baseball.

The baseball? At least as good as high-level U.S. college ball or even some AA Minor League. The players ranged from the late teens to early thirties. They had jobs, but how much work could they have done, what with games almost every day? Not the first time that sports have transcended the push for production that follows a revolution. The fielding was impressive—fast hands. The hitting and pitching were adequate.

The next day's paper neatly handled the Managua win, noting that its third baseman, Nelson Castro, had gone from "villano" to "héroe." Castro's error had let León go up early. But his bases-loaded double to left center shoved Managua ahead for good. The headline began: "Castro limpia bases..." Castro cleans the bases.

The game ended by 12:30 PM. The teams left in buses and the fans drifted away, heading to bus stops. I kept

"Baseball Brings Together All Segments of Society" by Eugene Novogrodsky. *The Barre-Montpelier Times Argus*, March 18, 1984. Reprinted with permission.

Baseball. Photo by Victor Sanchez.

thinking I was in Boston or Philadelphia in the 1920s—when baseball was part of fans' lives, not just another event on the entertainment slate.

The brigadistas—psyched by their practice the day before—played two baseball games with Nicaraguans who worked on the state-owned cotton farm. The Nicaraguans took the first game seriously and won 9–2. The second game, shortened by darkness, was a surprise—a 3–2 brigadista win.

I caught six innings in the 9–2 loss and then four more in the 3–2 win. No one else wanted to catch (only equipment was a glove and mask). I hadn't caught hard ball in more than twenty-five years and hadn't played any hard ball in more than fifteen. But softball isn't the rage in Nicaragua— baseball or nothing—so baseball it was.

Nicaraguans would stop tractors, join the game two innings, and then jump back on the tractors. Nicaraguan cotton pickers took two hours off to play baseball. Crop- dusting pilots took a break from their flights, left their planes, and walked by to see the action. Some of the militia played, leaning their rifles against a wooden fence and then reclaiming them after a turn in the field or at bat.

The weather: dry, windy, and hot. The scene: cotton fields beyond the outfielders. And: a backstop, dugouts, bleachers, grass infield, informal bases, rough mound, and sunken home plate.

I kept thinking I was in Vermont's venerable Country Mountain League, say a Danville–Chelsea game.

Some Nicaraguan sports notes:

Articles on running, boxing, basketball, soccer, ping-pong, and bicycle racing dot the three daily papers' sports sections. But baseball articles rule. Baseball became popular when the marines occupied Nicaragua several times from 1900 through the early 1930s.

Nicaraguan girls and women have years of catching up to do in the sports world. Little boys resist equal opportunity for the girls, even in kick-the-soccer-ball games.

I spent a half day taking buses around Managua to find a sporting goods store where I bought bats and balls with brigadista-donated money for another brigade to take to the cotton farm. Bats and balls were made in Nicaragua. Other baseball equipment in the store was Cuban-made.

Nicaraguan teen-age boys know a lot about U.S. athletes. They like the Orioles. Those boys, when they weren't laughing at the brigadistas' baseball efforts (my throwing error that let in two runs amused them and so did the left fielder robbing me of a hit), talked about three Nicaraguans who are in the majors: Cardinal David Green, Oriole Dennis Martinez, and Twin Al Williams.

Some final thoughts:

Sports, while often bitter and divisive, can also be pleasant and harmonious. The brigadistas and Nicaraguans got close thanks to sports, and sports might also be useful in bringing the governments of the United States and Nicaragua closer to peace—and thus further from a Central American war.

Naomi

Making love in Nicaragua Libre
with someone that speaks a different language
Two internationalist brigadistas
brought together by political idealism
In my arms
someone who took as much risk
as I
You live thousands of miles away
from Nicaragua Libre
and me

Free spirited and carefree
three days of touches
that would never be again
honesty was a natural
for why lie to someone
that will only be next to you
for a flash of your lifetime

Gentle caresses
soft moist kisses
waking up next to
an earthy sweaty carpenter
those three cool mornings
was heaven

Riding under the stars
in the back of a kind Nicaraguan's
pickup truck

Speaking of our experiences
in San Juan del Sur
and Apascalí

Hand holding
in Plaza de la Revolución

Singing "Good Day Sunshine"
down the block of the hospedaje
that gave us a night to remember
Making love over and over
each time more luscious
more precious

Thank you
for opening up
the dangerous and
free spirited side
of me.

Sofia Sequenzia

My attempt to visit Nicaragua and pick cotton with a
brigade turned into an adventure in a Soviet hospital in
Chinandega. I had been on the farm, Apascalí, only a full
day and had worked in the cotton fields a single morning.
On the way to a Sunday beach outing with my brigade and
the Nicaraguans from our farm, Angela (a fourteen-year-
old Nicaraguan girl) and I were seriously injured in a truck
accident.

Over sixty of us had set off on a flat-bed tractor-trailer,
usually used to transport bales of cotton but also needed to

transport people. As we began the descent on the road to the ocean, I could feel the tractor speeding, slipping gears, and losing its brakes. We had no sides to hold onto and, as a result, many of us fell off.

Through a well-coordinated effort by the brigadistas and the Nicaraguans, Angela and I were quickly transported by pick-up truck, on mostly unpaved roads, to the nearest hospital, two hours away. Angela died within thirty minutes of our arrival at the hospital. Her scalp was severed and she had lost much blood. I survived a fractured pelvis, bruised kidneys, internal bleeding, and later an attack of malaria.

The name "Hospital Sovietico" had no meaning for me until we arrived at the hospital. I found myself hearing Spanish spoken with a Russian accent in an enclave of Russian doctors, nurses, and aides. They dealt with our arrival as with any medical emergency, swiftly and thoroughly. My being North American was a novelty to them but irrelevant in terms of their treating me. The medical team was attentive and concerned about my health and comfort throughout my six-week stay. Although I had a primary doctor, numerous doctors monitored my progress. Despite the scarcity of space, they generously allowed a friend of mine, also a brigadista, to sleep in my room and care for me during that time.

With my hospital bed sandwiched between the operating rooms and the intensive care unit, I was privy to the comings and goings of the Russians, to their interactions with the Nicaraguan aides who assisted them, and to their work as a medical team. More than once I witnessed their ability to stay calm in the face of frequent power failures while operating and their intense efforts to revive dying patients.

This Soviet–Nicaraguan Friendship Hospital was established in 1982 after severe flooding devastated the area. The Soviet Union responded to the Nicaraguan plea for help and fully staffed and financed a hospital in what had once been a private clinic. Their contract has been renewed yearly, and the Soviet Hospital has become well known throughout Nicaragua for its excellent medical care. In 1983 alone, the Soviets treated more than 67,000 patients.

Close to sixty Soviets do one year of voluntary service in the hospital under difficult conditions. From my conversations with them, I surmised that they come for a variety of reasons, from good pay to a desire to travel to a genuine eagerness to help Nicaragua. The hospital, in addition to its 160-bed capacity, is a sprawling affair of canvas tents where Nicaraguans also receive ambulatory care and where the Russians eat and sleep. It is unbearably hot, and there is dust everywhere.

Despite the discomforts, the Russians worked hard, played hard (there was a volleyball game every day at 5 PM), partied hard (I often heard music, dancing, and singing in the night), and ate and drank heartily. I have memories of pairs of Russians playing chess under the shade by their tents and the young kitchen help peeling mountains of potatoes for lunch and dinner, while listening to Russian rock music.

My Nicaraguan doctor once said to me, "Soviets, not normal, they work, they work." They saw their role as professionals and were intent on providing their services, to the exclusion of integrating themselves into their new environment. They were not in Nicaragua to discuss internal politics or to impose their views.

On the other hand, the Nicaraguan aides and nurses, who also cared for me, were my eyes and ears to Nicaragua. My Nicaraguan experience was limited by my four walls and whoever entered there. We discussed everything from food to clothes to skin color, Somoza, the revolution, prostitution, machismo, babies, marriage, American music, and on. Together we laughed and puzzled over our similarities and differences—North American, Nicaraguan, and Russian—but feeling a mutual affection, interest, and respect as people.

Pensamientos de Apascalí

I inhale dust during a mid noon siesta
children running playing laughing
brown women constantly cooking
Nicaragua, land of the free/home of the brave

The heat is stagnant, a breeze brings dirt
and the smell of the latrines
cotton cotton everywhere
my mind wanders
to those soft white tufts
so natural
to be worn on foreign bodies

The smell of frijoles and tortillas
The barking of the dog
the oink of the pig
the occasional truck wanders by
bringing men, bringing sweet bread
bringing up dirt

In the crevices
of the wooden board I slept on
I left my bourgeois consciousness
and acquired
a newfound tolerance
carefree

Smile Yadel
throw the ball to me

children swarming our area
these children love to play
Yadel's brown hair bleached blond
by the hot sun
such a fresh little smirk
so in touch with nature naked
Damaris constantly being the
very young mother to her brother
Concern, discipline
all wrapped up in a frail girl's body
hair unkempt
awe at my shell earrings

love in her eyes

love in

Nicaragua

Teresa Sosa

When we got to Apascalí, about 150 people from the Maura Clarke Brigade had been there for two weeks. About 30 of them stayed, and I came with another 20.

*Did you spend any time with the Juventud,
the Sandinista youth?*

There was a student brigade up at Punta Ñata. We spent the fiftieth anniversary of Sandino's assassination with them. They were chanting. I saw all these young people, and I thought, my god, they are so much different from young people in our country. Maybe it was similar in the 60s. They were twelve, seventeen, twenty—my age. They had so much verve, so much energy for the revolution.

It had just been announced that the voting age had been lowered to sixteen. They were so happy. Here they were defending their country, and now they would also be able to vote. We had a dance. It was the dry season, so we were dancing in a cloud of dust. Bodies moving and dirt moving.

You speak Spanish. Do you feel you were able to really get to know them?

I would ask people different questions. And they would say, "Oh wow, you're Spanish, where are you from?" And I

Sandinista youth brigade heads for the cotton fields at Punta Ñata. Photo by Victor Sanchez.

would tell them, I'm half Puerto Rican and half Dominican. And they would say, "Oh, Puerto Rican, we have to free Puerto Rico!"

Have you maintained contact with any of the people you met there?

I've tried, but it's hard. One young woman I met was a teacher. She is in the militia. I fear that she's been mobilized to the front, and that's why she hasn't written to me. Sometimes I think, "Why isn't she writing." You know, I have this selfish sort of North American attitude. Then I think, "She's defending her country." I worry every time I hear of a contra attack, I think she's been hurt or killed. I want to go back and find her. I felt a real connection with her.

She had a little child that she left behind with her mother in order to come up there and teach. It was the first school they had ever had there. Registration was going on while we were there. She was trying to get all the mothers to bring their little kids to register.

Were the children excited?

Some were very excited. They were getting paper and pens, and they were going to be able to write. It was a whole new experience for them. The teacher would make them wear shoes, try to educate them about disease. It's frustrating to think she would have to leave and go to fight.

There was an accident at my farm. A flatbed truck went down a hill, and it didn't have any brakes. One of the North Americans was hurt. She had to spend two months in the Soviet hospital. A young Nicaraguan woman died in that same accident. They couldn't get her to the hospital in time. This girl's little brother had died during the previous brigade.

Then I began to make connections. The reason why the truck went down the hill without brakes was because there weren't enough spare parts. Most of the trucks are U.S. made and the U.S. has an embargo on spare parts. This young woman died because of what the U.S. is doing to Nicaragua. I remember crying for her, because she was younger than I am.

Kit Miller

Dear Friends:

I wish you could've seen my brigade! There were 200 of us there the last two weeks of February, and it was great to hear the introductions on the first day. There were farmers, union folks, computer workers, veterans, professionals, older people, and students. Most are doing something in their hometowns (they were from all over the States) to stop U.S. intervention—from teach-ins to letter writing campaigns to press work to holding up signs on freeways. I gained a lot of respect for these folks—they have great senses of humor as well as spirit and commitment.

In the few days we spent near Managua before hitting the cotton fields we had many adventures.

Managua

It is an eye opener in itself to go to Managua. There's no real downtown; in fact much of the city is bare fields and empty lots. That's because the earthquake of '72 destroyed so many buildings. When massive international aid poured in, Somoza stuck the money in his Swiss bank accounts. That was when most of the middle class began to sympathize with the growing revolution. It's hard to tell which buildings were destroyed by the earthquake and which by Somoza's bombings just before he fled the country.

We also see reminders of the new threat to Nicaragua. In each neighborhood the community organizations have dug trenches—six feet deep, fifteen to twenty-five feet long. These are where the people will hide if the country is invaded. Since the U.S. invasion of Grenada, Nicaraguans have dug thousands of these trenches throughout their country.

Getting in and around Managua takes some doing. Buses and trucks are extremely crowded—the government estimates that it needs 600 more vehicles to meet basic transportation needs. Because it's poor, because it can't get international loans, and because of Somoza's legacy of destruction, much of Nicaragua's infrastructure is in similar disarray—phones don't work, mail takes a month from the States, John Deere tractors sit rusting in the fields for lack of parts. These inconveniences are a source of some irritation to us foreigners. They are a way of life to Nicaragua.

Ciudad Sandino

Bouncing on the bus to one of the poorest barrios outside Managua. The old man beside me alternates between suspicion—"Why are you here? Are you communists?" —and a grandfatherly pat on the knee. He yells, "It's one thing to visit a poor country, and another to live here!" "Go back to your President Reagan, and tell him we want peace." We meet people with varied opinions about the new government, but all of them tell us they want to work out their own problems.

We disembark and walk down the dusty street past Casa de Cultura Victor Jara (named for the Chilean folksinger murdered by the military following the 1973 coup).

Elvis and Jesus, Managua, Nicaragua. Photo by Kevin Gerien.

There are community notices tacked up beside the walk. From the youth, "We are constructing the new country— we want to vote!" From the women's organizations, "In building the new country, we forge the new woman. Participate in the regional assembly of militia women. Free country or die!" And from the government, "Parents—bring your children for polio vaccination! February 12."

A mother of many beckons us into her one room tortilla factory, where six kids help cook and grind corn. She is happy with the progress in the neighborhood—electricity has been brought in, and paving. They are still working on bringing in plumbing. Youths down the street yell at us from the site where they're reconstructing the fire station that was bombed during the Final Days. They stand proudly on the skeletal structure, as we snap their pictures.

Masaya

Touring through this bullet- and grafitti-riddled town. Past the church where charismatics rock out and the plaster Jesus lies in state staring up at the holey gold ceiling.

We find the mask factory, where a lone mask-maker hammers out mesh faces on a wooden form. He welcomes us and takes time to explain the history of the creepy faces. Originally, they were worn by local Indians, who dressed up in Spanish drag and imitated the conquistadores in dances. This has been continued as part of a Catholic saint's day. But the masks really made a comeback during the Revolution, when the young rebels wore them to hide their identities from the National Guard. According to the mask maker, they would grab the mask from its place on the wall, run out to do an action, and replace it afterwards. Interesting to think about the role of the masks in relation to the various rulers.

We stumble across the Museum of Heroes and Martyrs. After hearing that we are "brigadistas," an old man warmly invites us on a tour of the exhibit. It is mostly photographs of Masayans who fell in battle against the Guard (heroes), or who were captured, raped or tortured, and killed (martyrs). Starting with a few 1930 cowboy compañeros of Sandino, the pictures quickly move into late '70s formal high school shots of boys and girls. His explanations are brief—"This group was hiding in a basement. They were betrayed and the Guard threw in a bomb." "This group of doctors and nurses were tending comrades in the hospital. The Guard came, took them out and shot them, then threw gasoline on the patients inside and set them on fire." "There is now a hospital named after this nurse who was raped and killed by the Guard."

It is surreal, imagining these scrubbed young faces (sometimes ten or twelve years old!) hidden behind mesh masks, running messages, making up a contact bomb, building barricades, found dead.

Soledad—A Farm Near León

Finally the cotton picking day arrives! We load onto buses and head for León. Our cotton farm is Soledad, fifteen kilometers outside town. En route we pass billboards advertising fertilizers and community notices pushing for increased production.

A Day in the Life—Soledad

Up at 4:30—Scorpio is giant in the clear sky. Fumble for your clothes and bowl and file past the huge pot of beans and rice and tortillas (the cook women have been up since 3:30!). Scarf it down, don your cotton-sack, hat, kerchief, grab your water bottle (are they all full?), and out to the field. The sun rises across the fields and fields of fat white cotton. The distant volcano is smoking and red in the morning light.

Six o'clock and pick, pick, pick. We get the picked-over-by-machine fields so there's less on them. But cotton is still all around and over us. Talk and sing and make jokes and meditate on *cotton*. And drink lots of water. *Heat and dust* and bright sun. After three and a half hours, our sacks are full, shoulders sore, and we go in for weighing. Most of us pick thirty pounds per day.

At Night—Soledad Farm

A cultural exchange with the Nicaraguan campesinos. We juggle, sing Nicaraguan songs, U.S. union songs, read poetry. They watch impassively. A beautiful young black woman recites Holly Near's Lifeline song about Harriet Tubman. "Last night I dreamed I was in slavery..." and improvises a dance while it is translated. The evening winds up with two brigadista women demonstrating self-defense, throwing each other on the ground. Nicas and gringos

Brigadistas participating in blockade of U.S. Federal Building to protest Reagan administration policies in Central America, June 9, 1984. Photo by Kevin Gerien.

share amazement as one psyches herself up and with her fist breaks an inch-thick board! Wild applause from both cultures.

February 21

The fiftieth anniversary of Sandino's assassination. It is a big holiday, and the entire nation goes to Managua—except us. Though many of us would give our cotton-pickin' right arms to be there, the logistical nightmare of lugging 100 brigadistas to a crowded demo and finding them again at the end is more than our hosts can face. Besides, we've only been at the farm two days and hardly deserve a break! So we pick in the morning and crowd around the farm radio to hear Daniel Ortega announce the upcoming Nicaraguan elections. They are to be November 4, two days before ours! We try to figure all the consequences—definitely moving the election to two months earlier than originally planned is a good move. Hopefully Reagan won't invade Nicaragua before their elections—that would appear undemocratic!! And that might make him look bad for his own reelection. Election on Sunday is a nice touch—everyone can vote.

Editor's Note—The Contra

The purpose of the contras is to disrupt the Nicaraguan economy, to eliminate the positive accomplishments of the Sandinista revolution, and to terrorize the population. In 1984, more than 3,000 Nicaraguans were victims of the contras. Of those, 1,600 were killed—more than 4 Nicaraguans a day—and the rest either wounded, mutilated, or kidnapped. Of those murdered, more than 100 were children below the age of twelve. In 1984, the contras caused 254.9 million dollars of material damage through the month of November, an amount that represents more than 70 percent of that year's export earnings.

The contras are led by ex-Somoza National Guardsmen but include some former Nicaraguan revolutionaries. They have added to their numbers by recruiting and kidnapping young peasants from the northern provinces.

How did this situation develop? In his first days in office, President Reagan ordered the CIA to begin rebuilding its covert action capabilities. In March 1981, he ordered the CIA to develop a broad political action effort in Latin America. In November 1981, he issued a directive ordering the CIA to "assist" in developing an anti-Sandinista guerrilla army. The CIA's program was initially called "La Tripartita." The three parts, according to the *Wall Street Journal* (March 5, 1985), were "...American money, Argentine trainers and Honduran territory" combined in order to ".... create a guerrilla army known as the Fuerza Democratica Nicaragüense, or FDN." The FDN, along with ARDE (the Democratic Revolutionary Alliance), MISURA (referring to the Miskitu, Suma, and Rama native peoples), and MISU-RASATA, another native organization, have become known collectively as the contras. In Nicaragua, it is common to refer to the counterrevolution simply as the contra.

CULTURAL WORKERS BRIGADE
August 5–26, 1984

Under Somoza our cultural capital was Miami Beach.

Ernesto Cardenal
Nicaraguan Minister of Culture

Jeffry Steele

¡Internacionalismo es...Revolución!

We are a group of ten artists and eleven musicians from the United States, the Artists' Brigade for the New Nicaragua—the first of what we hope will be many cultural brigades to that country. Based on the same idea as the coffee and cotton brigades—which have been organized by solidarity associations in Europe and the U.S. to assist the tireless people and the battered economy of Nicaragua in these labor-intensive harvests—the Artists' Brigade was assembled by Arts for a New Nicaragua, a committee of people based in Boston who have experience doing cultural work in Nicaragua. Recognizing the need not only for materials, but also for instruction, Arts for a New Nicaragua invited a variety of professional musicians and artists to form a brigade, working through the Sandinista government's Ministry of Culture.

In Nicaragua our brigade was coordinated by Sonia Cano, who heads international relations in the national office of the Centers for Popular Culture (CPC). In her mid-thirties, she has five children: two living at home with her, two studying in Cuba, and one stationed at the front. The three of us who preceded the arrival of the brigade by three weeks in order to facilitate preparations were amazed and inspired by our first meeting with Sonia in which she explained the vision and expectations the CPC had developed for our trip. The painters were not simply to paint murals; they were to work with Nicaraguans developing mural designs and imparting techniques. The musicians were not coming just to entertain and give a few lessons; we were to be sent to military installations, to hospitals, and to conduct

Mural painted by North American cultural workers and Nicaraguan artists in León. Photo by Anthony Yarus.

a five-day seminar for the music teachers brought specially together from nearly every region of the country.

Nicaraguan songs we heard generally fell into two categories: romantic and testimonial—the latter describing personal experience with the revolutionary process. Though there appeared to be a limited number of stock strums and picking patterns in use, Nicaraguan singing was never limited in its intensity or passion. One of the tragedies I witnessed was seeing very talented musicians playing horrible instruments—they can't *get* decent guitars.

The Sandinista government places an unheard-of emphasis on cultural activities. One might well expect—in a country trying to pull itself back together after a revolutionary war and struggling with economic sanctions, trade embargoes, and mercenary attacks—that cultural work would receive an understandably low priority. But we are talking about a government many of whose leaders are poets or writers; a government that came to power through a grass-roots movement beginning in religious communities and schools; a government whose first major decree, once in power, prompted thousands of volunteers who could read and write to journey to the farthest corners of the country to instruct those who couldn't; a government that, having now also learned from its mistakes in the Miskitu territory, respects and actually promotes the indigenous culture of each region. One of my students in the music seminar spoke proudly of how the regional CPC at which he teaches is better funded than many of the others because it is located in a coffee-growing area under contra attack. The Sandinistas realize that their strength comes not from ammunition alone.

Rikki Asher

Sandinista ideology says that the development of a people's culture is as important as the development of industry and defense. Before the revolution, only the rich had access to culture. Today, great emphasis is placed on reclaiming cultural heritage and opening new avenues of creativity, even during this time of escalating military threats.

Following the fall of Somoza on July 19, 1979, all the social clubs that had been for the private use of his friends were taken over and transformed into Centers for Popular Culture.

I went to Granada with two other artists. Our work base was the CPC, where we stored materials and first met with members of the women's group AMNLAE. They were

Mural detail and street scene. Photo by Rikki Asher.

very excited about the idea of painting a mural. They helped us every day.

Our first project was to complete a mural that the Nicaraguan artist Nicasio Del Castillo could not finish because he ran out of paint. As we prepared the wall, crowds of people came by daily to watch. They commented, questioned, and helped with the painting. The core group were the women from AMNLAE and children from the area.

The central image of the mural is a woman, representing the mothers of Nicaragua, her son by her side carrying the FSLN flag, with a border of lush flowers and leaves. We asked for help naming the mural and it became "Madre y Hijo Construyendo Nuestra Patria!" (Mother and Son Build Our Country!).

Our second project was in Jinotepe, a town south of Managua and west of Granada. The wall we chose was fifty-three feet by eighteen feet. It had been part of a Shell gas station. Our discussion about the role of women since the revolution became the theme for this mural. The images include women as mothers, as educators, as doctors, as factory workers, and as fighters. We also researched the traditional Indian motifs of Nicaraguan designs and used a repetitive pattern for the border. Marvin Campos, a mural painter from Jinotepe, worked with us. The title is "Mural A AMNLAE Jinotepe." Within the mural is a banner with the words, "Para la defensa del futuro las mujeres seguimos de frente con el Frente—AMNLAE," meaning, "In defense of the future of women, we go with the FSLN."

Willie Sordill

One of my most moving experiences in Nicaragua came at our second performance, at a military police training school just outside of Managua. It had been a day of plans changed many times over and long waiting for transportation to the rescheduled performance. By the time we arrived in two small vehicles, I was tired and did not have particularly high expectations for the performance. The conditions were not what I had come to assume were necessary for optimal performing. There would be no warm-up time, no sound system in an outdoor setting, no real back-stage to compose oneself. And we would be singing primarily in English to a non-English-speaking audience!

As we disembarked from our vehicles and walked through a doorway directly onto a platform that would serve as the stage, the soldiers standing in wait in the concrete and asphalt courtyard directly below began to clap for us. It was not polite applause, but thunderous, spirited applause that welcomed and appreciated our appearance as if we were old friends. It was a passionate applause that would have moved me almost to tears if it had come at the end of a performance. It had an even more dramatic effect as we stood face to face, applauding each other before ever having played a note. The applause soon gave way to a series of consignas, with a lone initiator yelling out a part of a phrase to a thunderous unison response. Our favorite was, "Cultura es... fusil artístico de la revolución!" "Culture is an artistic weapon of the revolution."

The applause and chants that continued to fill every available space during our arrival and the unpacking of our equipment remained at such a spirited fervor that I feared that our performance would be a let-down; it would have been a difficult level of energy to maintain for a high-powered and experienced performing ensemble, and here we were at what would be only our second performance together. And as I gazed out over the audience and into the open eyes of the soldiers, some of whom leaned comfortably against one another or rested a forearm on a compañero's shoulder casually, I felt like I could see and feel history, struggle, determination, suffering, a will to go on in a way I had never experienced before. I learned more from what I

read in their eyes at that moment than I could have from ten volumes of Latin American history. And as I stood at the back of the stage watching as Laura and Roger sang "We Are Free," there was no way in the world to stop the tears from streaming down my face.

Willie Sordill

Dulio, Cleo and Sonia

Dear Dulio, how are you my friend?
Here is the music I promised to send you
Sorry it took so long but you know
It's been busy here and the mail is so slow
Do you remember that night we spent out on the street
In front of your house until a quarter to three?
You played guitar and I played the sax
And all the neighbors came out—but they weren't mad
They sang along, they all sang along
Tell your mother hello, I miss her cooking
And the talks we had in the morning

Dear Cleo, how have you been my sister?
I wish I could be there to see you dance
But by the time you receive this I'll have missed my chance
Hope it went well, I know it went well
I think of that restaurant in Estelí
You sat at the table with David and me
I still hear your laugh, it rings like a choir

When you speak of freedom your eyes turn to fire
Just like when you dance, like when you dance
And by the way
Thanks for taking my letters to Sonia

Dear Sonia, hola mi amor, I hope you're well
You are my first thought when I open my eyes
You're the last thing I think of when I lay down at night
And all the time in between

And though I hold your letter still it doesn't seem real
I touch the pink paper made brown by the fields
I close my eyes and catch the smell of your hair
And try to believe you once lay next to me there
But it seems less real than a dream

Last night I read the paper as I lay in my bed
Wide-awake nightmares circled my head
I could see you in the dawn in the cool mountain air
In the shadow of an airplane that shouldn't have been there
And it's Christmas eve
And all I want is for you to be alive for Christmas

And I love you much more than these words can say
Don't think it's just my Spanish

Willie Sordill

I Don't Know

Sit at the table with Sonia
So full of life it blinds to look in her eyes
Shiny black hair and a smile that conceals
So many years fighting bullets and lies
She's no faceless stranger
And if she were the crime would be as great
No faceless stranger—she's a friend that I love
But there's a gun at her head and I can't stand by and wait
And if the bombs come down on Managua
If the Marines once again hit the shore

I don't know
I just don't know
I don't know but I just might pick up a gun

It's not the British with their polite ways
Their neat little uniforms and sense of fair play
These are Somoza's Guards who not long ago
Pushed men and women from their planes into hungry
    volcanoes
Up in León the writing on the prison wall
Says, "Here lies Mariano; over there you'll find his balls"
I know you don't like to hear this; I've gone too far
Well someone has for sure and they used more than a guitar
And I've got news for you—I hate to sing this song
And I won't write a new verse next time
Cause it's gone on too long
And I don't know
And I just don't know
I don't know but I just might pick up a gun

I think myself a man of peace
Never saw a difference 'tween ends and means
Marched round the Pentagon too many times
Seen the inside of a jail for singing on a picket line
Wrote off to Congress and read the replies
Watched each commission print up the same lies
Meanwhile the most peaceful ones I've ever seen
Laugh and love and make sure their guns are clean
If they carried signs instead, just how far d'you think
    they'd get?—
While CIA supplies the Contras and we politely protest
And I don't know
I just don't know
I don't know but I just might pick up a gun

Debra Wise

Puppetry in the New Nicaragua

There are twenty-two of us, mostly from New England, a few from New York and California. Half of us are visual artists, half are musicians. We have been invited by the Nicaraguan Ministry of Culture to come as the first working brigade of artists from North America. Sonia Cano, our hostess and a director of international relations for the ministry, tells us immediately upon our arrival, "Your stay here will not be temporary, but permanent"; that is to say, our job is not only to do our own work, but to paint murals, make music, and share our skills with Nicaraguan artists. Being the only puppeteer in the group, my job is cut out for me; I've brought along "Tillie," a red-headed hand-and-rod puppet that has become a kind of alter ego. Besides performing for two weeks, I'll be teaching a week-long seminar on shadow puppetry.

Our trip was sponsored by the Centers for Popular Culture, an important part of what the Nicaraguans call the "democratization of culture." Community art centers are opening all over the country, so local people can see performances, take classes, and develop pride in their own culture by helping to reshape it. We performed in schools, churches, factories, parks, and hospitals, at religious festivals, for unions and women's organizations, and for the military. We were even on Sandinista television, after which children on the street would all recognize my puppet whenever I pulled her out of my knapsack. "Titere! Titere!" they would call. Tillie was very useful for me, in ways I hadn't expected. I had been very nervous about my Spanish, which is terrible. But my puppet could blame me for her bad Spanish, and somehow that made it all right. Her running joke was that she had learned that the Nicaraguan government had given up being a puppet, and she had come to Central America to see how she could do the same thing. Then she would play on her kazoo trombone a very popular romantic song, "Ah, Nicaragua, Nicaragüita" (little Nicaragua), "the most beautiful flower that I love...as sweet as honey...but now that you are free, Nicaragüita, I love you even more." She was a big hit.

There had been no puppetry in Nicaragua before the revolution. While I was there, I attended the opening of the new National Workshop for Puppetry in the beautiful mountain town of Matagalpa. It will be a retreat for artists to come to study and to work on new pieces. The buildings, simple and serviceable, were constructed with the help of people from Belgium, Germany, and Holland. At the celebration, in fact, there were many "Internacionalistas," so many that children made it into a kind of game, running up and guessing, "Sueca? Francesa? Italiana? Norteamericana?" Even the director of puppet programs for the Centers for Popular Culture, Juan Espinoza, is from abroad. He is from Bolivia and was touring outside the country when a military coup erupted. He decided to make Nicaragua his home. The Assistant Minister of Culture, Francisco Lacayo, told us at a press conference, "Nicaragua is very small, but there is room here for all the world."

At the celebration, I saw a puppet, mask, and actor play by the Nistayolero Theater (an Indian word meaning "light of tomorrow"). The main puppet figure is a giant peasant woman who represents the Nicaraguan people. The parable they performed, set in Spanish colonial times, was about a priest who is a friend of the people but is betrayed by a "mestizo" (half-Spanish, half-Indian), who misrepresents the priest as a traitor. This much was clear, but when I was trying to explain to Juan what I thought the other parts of the story "meant," he shook his head and said that I shouldn't analyze so much, that really much of the play was pure poetry. This proved to be the case for most of the art I enjoyed in Nicaragua: the themes are political. "We have to make art about change," I was told, "because so much change is necessary" (but the art is poetic).

My students were all working puppeteers, on salary from the Ministry of Culture to develop their craft. They had never seen or made shadow puppets before and were very enthusiastic; they produced wonderful puppets, some using cardboard, others experimenting with clear plastic and acetate inks. We played with different light sources, flames, mirrors, prisms, and an old overhead projector I had brought along to leave as a donation (a tool that is easy for us to find here but impossible for them to afford).

After the seminar, I interviewed my students and asked them to tell me more about themselves. Some of them were from a company that usually works for television. They were already making plans to air a shadow-puppet play about Sandino's life. It was interesting to watch their director, Gonzalo Cuellas Leano, also from Bolivia, as we discussed their work. He kept deferring to the younger members of the company, clearly trying to help them develop their abilities to articulate their work. They explained that they had been sent to the countryside as part of a cultural brigade, where they performed a hand-puppet play called "The Thief in the Neighborhood," designed to encourage people to cooperate and share the country's limited resources. The puppeteers were especially appreciated in the small towns in the beautiful but dangerous northern regions of the country. The puppeteers had to learn to defend themselves. They were told to carry guns at all times, like the farmers in the countryside have to do. They admitted to taking them off, however, when they performed. Not only were the guns uncomfortable, but they discovered that they could keep the puppets from getting dirty by putting the guns in the mud and the puppets on top! Something any street puppeteer can appreciate.

The other puppeteers in my class were from a company that works for the Centers for Popular Culture. They have a different kind of mission; they also perform, but they primarily teach puppetry to community volunteers and social service workers. They are especially interested in working with children. You often hear adults say that they have the responsibility of rebuilding their country for the sake of the children. One of my students, Solema, is an elementary teacher who was selected by the Ministry of Education to work for a year as a puppeteer. She will learn the techniques and then go back and apply them in an educational program. Their main goal is to counteract the years of hardship and violence by putting into the hands of children the tools they need to become expressive, creative adults.

I asked my students what kind of help they needed in their work. They need so many basic tools, impossible to get in Nicaragua: scissors, razor knives, wire snips, needle-nose pliers, clip lights, hole punches, steel nails, masking tape, film, cassettes, books in Spanish about puppet techniques. I took notes furiously, thinking about how I could help send trunks of donations to my new friends. But they stopped me. "Really," they said, "on the other hand, our lack of materials helps us to use our imaginations, to develop puppetry into a popular art form here."

Rosemarie Straijer

We arrived in León in the late afternoon. Our performance had been scheduled for 2 PM, but, because of trouble getting transportation from Managua, our bus pulled into this charming town at nearly 5 PM. A small crowd had

Nicaraguan militia members visit with North American friend in front of a mural painted by U.S. artists on the wall of a León firehouse. Photo by Anthony Yarus.

gathered on the street where we were expected in front of the AMNLAE office, a women's organization named in honor of Luisa Amanda Espinosa, the first woman to die in combat against Somoza.

Our one-hour performance was well received, Debra's puppet the hit of the evening. Our artistic sensibilities extremely satisfied, we packed away our instruments into our "vehiculo" and were led away from our performance site. Sonia, our leader, guided us to a place where we could be fed—the home of an old woman who had opened her place as a "comedor" (eating place) for students from the University of León years ago. As we walked toward her house, our group of six musicians, three muralists, and two Nicaraguans in the lead spread out over the small and relatively unbusy streets of León. The doors and windows to many of the homes we walked past were open. Beautiful tile floors, very high ceilings, at least two majestic rocking chairs (which are made there), and, most significantly, two or even three deep rooms extending inward toward the back of the house.

That sense of depth and space was not without purpose, as I later found out. We sat in the living room awaiting our food (starving quietly of course). The old woman who ran the house sat quietly in her rocking chair, observing all these "internacionalistas." Sonia began explaining to me the history of León—its people, traditions, and involvement in the revolutionary struggles of Nicaragua.

Sonia was raised in León as a child, so the history she was about to tell me was part of her own experience growing up. León, she said, is an extremely conservative town. As a youngster she recalls that most families kept their doors and windows shut in order to maintain their privacy. This is rare in tropical Nicaragua. More than anywhere else in this land of lakes and volcanoes, in León people believe in magic. If something can't be explained, it is attributed to magic.

During the final revolutionary insurrection in July 1979, León's conservative populace surprised everyone. They proved themselves to be true combatientes (fighters for the revolution). They were every bit as ready to stand up for themselves and the free country they envisioned as everyone else in the country was. León was the first town in Nicaragua to be taken by the Sandinistas. By the time this insurrection occurred, the people knew exactly what they were doing. They had set up a clandestine network that linked those homes with the deep corridors and layers of rooms. Built closely together, the homes served as hideouts for large numbers of civilians escaping the Guardia Nacional. They escaped by fleeing from one house to the next. The National Guard would see them in one spot, chase them down, and the small crowd would disappear "magically" through the back rooms of one house into the next, and the next, and the next.

This amazing town lives beyond these historic moments, though not without its reminders. Many buildings still remain with mortar holes in their walls. The townspeople still believe in magic, and as we left León I could see why.

MARVIN JOSE LOPEZ REFORESTATION BRIGADE

September 9–October 7, 1984

Ric Mohr

Richard W. Franke

Testimony on Nicaragua
Presented to the New Jersey Citizens
Investigation of U.S. War Crimes in
Central America and the Caribbean

My name is Richard W. Franke. I am Professor of Anthropology at Montclair State College. From September 9
to October 7, 1984, I was in Nicaragua as a member of the
Marvin José Lopez Reforestation Brigade. The testimony
that I wish to submit is based primarily on my personal
observations as a member of this project. I am not an aca-
demic expert on Latin America, but my profession as an
anthropologist involves accurate and detailed reporting on
the nature of human social behavior. While in Nicaragua, I
took several hundred pages of notes in meetings and conversations with a wide variety of Nicaraguans of several
social categories and political orientations and made over
twenty-two hours of taped interviews. My testimony to
this investigation is based on these notes and interviews, as
well as eyewitness observations.

The New Jersey Citizens Investigation of U.S. War Crimes in
Central America and the Caribbean was one of thirteen tribunals held
by the National Conference of Black Lawyers, La Raza Legal Alliance,
the Center for Constitutional Rights, and the National Lawyers Guild
during the fall of 1984. Richard Franke's testimony was presented at the
Rutgers Law School, Newark, New Jersey on October 12, 1984. The
tribunals heard expert witnesses on the region and investigated U.S.
government violations of U.S. and international law. Further information and a copy of the *Judgment of the New York War Crimes Tribunal on
Central America and the Caribbean* can be obtained from the Central America Task Force, c/o the National Lawyers Guild, 853 Broadway, Room
1705, New York, New York 10003.

In addition to a few days in Managua, I was in the northern town of Estelí from September 11 to 16 and from September 17 to October 2 in the town of Somoto, fifteen kilometers from the Honduran border. My unique experience in Somoto in particular allowed me to see first hand some of the consequences of the U.S.-CIA "covert" war against Nicaragua.

Economic Sabotage of the Rural Economy of the Somoto Region

Our own tree-planting project experienced delays each morning in starting work because we had to wait several hours for the military to inspect and verify the safety of the road to our work site, only nine kilometers from the town. While Nicaraguans normally start work at 5:30 or 6:00 AM, in rural Madriz, where Somoto is located, we had to wait often until 8:00 or even 9:00 AM until word was received that the area was safe for passage to the work site.

Futher Economic Sabotage

All government workers in Somoto and many other citizens are required, because of the contra threats, to carry out what is called revolutionary vigilance. For some, this involves staying awake through the night in their home neighborhoods one to three nights each week. For others, it means patrolling the local hills one to three nights each week. These defense demands wear out workers and make more difficult their already overburdened lives.

Interference with Transport and Planning of Development Projects

Our own tree-planting project was to have worked for several days near the town of Ocotál, twenty kilometers north of Somoto. Because the road to Ocotál was not safe, we were never able to accomplish this work and, indeed, were not able even to visit the town.

Further Economic Sabotage

Rural villages in northern Nicaragua must be protected by trenches around the perimeters of the villages, and some even have full-time, heavy machine-gun positions established at opposite ends of the villages. This need for constant military preparedness and investment of time and equipment in defense represents a serious impediment to the reconstruction efforts since the Revolution and the longer term development of infrastructure and economic activity.

Physical Destruction

On the morning of September 23, 1984, contra forces attacked and destroyed the grain storage silos at Palacaquina, a small town eighteen kilometers from Somoto. Several residents of the town heard the explosion and reported it to us before it was announced on Nicaraguan radio. Later reports described the damage as follows: six silos destroyed with 90,000 kilograms of rice; 80,200 kilograms of corn; 27,400 kilograms of beans; 17,400 kilograms of salt, and 5,000 kilograms of soap. One defender of the silos was killed in the attack. On October 2, our group visited the site of the destruction and photographed the twisted remains of the silos and hundreds of torn and scattered bags of food and soap.

Further Physical Destruction

You are probably aware of the CIA–contra naval attack on the port city of Corinto on October 10, 1983, in which several thousand barrels of oil were destroyed. From Douglas Murray, a former California pesticide technical

Oil tanks destroyed in CIA-led bombing attack on the Port of Corinto, October 10, 1983. Photo by Paul Tick.

advisor to OSHA (Occupational Safety and Health Administration), now working with the Nicaraguan Ministry of Labor, I learned of further consequences of that attack. On the docks the day of the attack were large stores of the pesticide methylparathion, a relatively safe chemical that the Nicaraguans were planning to use to kill the boll weevil, the main insect pest attacking the cotton harvest. In the five years since the Revolution, the new government had reduced the use of more dangerous organochlorines that have been shown consistently in experiments in the U.S. to cause cancer in laboratory animals. In some cotton areas around León, women's breast milk had been tested and found to contain forty-two to forty-five times the maximum tolerance level for organochlorines as established by U.S. studies. The switch to methylparathion was thus crucial to Nicaragua's attempts to become one of the safest cotton producing countries in the Third World. Because the attack on Corinto occurred just as the cotton harvest was about to begin, and because nearly the entire imported supply of methylparathion was destroyed, the authorities were forced to use organochlorines. Five years of progress in improving the safety of cotton workers were undone in a single CIA attack.

Further Destruction and Economic Sabotage

On several days, our work brigade planted trees at the Asentamiento (settlement) Hermanos Martinez. This is a refugee camp of 180 families who were forced to abandon their isolated rural homes in the northern mountains because of the threat of contra attacks. After just a few months, the camp has a functioning school and an infant feeding center in which all children who have not completed sixth grade are given two nutritious meals per day, with much of the food donated by the European Economic Community. A health clinic has been started, but construction is delayed by a critical shortage of cement resulting from the war situation.

Physical Destruction of Nicaraguan People

Contra forces rarely attack army positions but focus on unarmed civilians and especially on government workers. Officials of the Nicaraguan Teachers' Union (ANDEN) in Somoto informed me that eighteen teachers had been killed by contras in the past three years, and that all rural teachers in the area have received death threats. Teachers must travel to their rural classrooms armed with automatic rifles and must teach their classes under fear of attack.

Further Killings

On September 23, 1984, contra forces ambushed an army truck near Pantasma, in the Jinotega area, killing eight mothers who were going to visit their sons in the army. According to information from local people, three troop trucks were allowed to pass before the contras opened fire on the women.

Further Killings

On September 29, 1984, the Sandinista newspaper *Barricada* and the independent newspaper *El Nuevo Diario* reported a contra attack on an isolated peasant family three kilometers southwest of the town of Chinandega. In this attack, three children were killed, one of them eleven months old, and an adult was wounded who lived to recount the story.

Further Killings

At least ten health inspectors of the Ministry of Labor have been killed by contras.

Kidnappings and Probable Further Killings

On the day I left Nicaragua, October 7, 1984, *Barricada* reported the kidnapping of five high school students near El Cua. The students were part of an educational brigade that is continuing the work begun in Nicaragua's adult literacy campaign.

Effects of Mobilization

The constant contra attacks have forced the mobilization of men and women from all walks of life. Douglas Murray stated that, of forty health and safety inspectors in the new government's pesticide monitoring program, thirteen have been mobilized for combat and another five have been called up for production brigades. This loss of eighteen of forty trained inspectors has set Nicaragua back years in its efforts to conduct research on the extent of pesticide absorption by rural workers and in the equally crucial task of referring workers for medical care and making recommendations on the withdrawal of harmful pesticides when evidence warrants.

Further Economic Sabotage

Outside the town of Somoto, we viewed and photographed a severely damaged propane truck. A time bomb had been inserted in the truck on the Honduran side of the border while the driver was filling out customs papers. When the truck arrived at the weigh station in Somoto, it exploded. Because of such attacks, Nicaragua has had to limit the importation of propane through Honduras, a major supply route. This in turn has forced many urban middle-class families to shift from propane to wood fire cooking, a serious short and long term environmental problem in a country where the forest cover has already been reduced far below the 30 percent level considered necessary by forestry experts. This environmental crisis developed through the 1950s and 1960s when the Somozas opened the forested mountains to intensive cutting by U.S.-based lumber companies.

Destruction of Towns

The border town of El Espino, fifteen kilometers from Somoto, had to be abandoned in 1983 because of constant mortaring from the Honduran side. The residents of El Espino have been resettled in a ramshackle suburb of Somoto. The former customs post at El Espino has been placed in a reinforced truck guarded by regular army troops. The truck goes to the border each day to check passports of tourists and others who enter the country and it returns at night to the greater safety of Somoto.

Constant Use of Weapons

One of the most dramatic pieces of evidence concerning the state of war in northern Nicaragua is that virtually the entire adult male population and much of the adult female population carry automatic rifles at all times. The passing out of arms to so many people raises the risk of accidental shootings, and I learned of a killing last February of one militia member by another in a fight over a woman in a cotton harvesting village on the Pacific coast. Such deaths and injuries occur from time to time; they are a by-product of the all-out mobilization that the country has been forced to undertake.

The Murder of Marvin José Lopez

I want to share with you the story behind the name of our reforestation brigade. On June 1, 1984, in the northern Nicaraguan town of Ocotál, twenty kilometers from where we stayed, a young forester named Marvin José Lopez was setting out in his Toyota truck to pick up workers to plant trees. It was 5 AM and no one in the truck was armed. On the edge of town, contra forces ambushed his vehicle, firing several rounds at nearly point-blank range. Lopez was killed instantly by a bullet that tore into the driver's side, while four other people were able to duck and survive.

The attackers ran after firing these first shots, but a dedicated and peaceful forester was lost to Nicaragua. Upon hearing of this crime against an unarmed environmentalist, we North Americans decided to name our project after him and to plant as many trees as possible. In all, we planted 26,000 trees this past month in Nicaragua.

Sesshu Foster

One Way To Get Nicaraguan Earth Under Your Fingernails

The Marvin José Lopez Brigade was a diverse group of people, aged nineteen to seventy-two. Some were activists in the solidarity movement, some had little experience with political activism and were coming for personal reasons.

Some of us had a good deal of experience with manual labor, like Paul, a seventy-two-year-old retired mineworker and union organizer. Others had almost none. Some of us were between jobs, having scraped up enough money to go with the help of our coworkers, family, and friends. There were Alex, a Puerto Rican from New York; Lupe and Teresa, two Chicanas from Fresno; Jay, who had been involved in antinuclear demonstrations in Denver; Ed, who edited an organic farming newsletter out of his farm in Ohio; Pratt, the son of the exmayor of Little Rock, Arkansas; Sue, a student from Ann Arbor; Ron, a tugboat deckhand from San Pedro; Terry, in the import–export business in Seattle. This diversity may have made for irritating discussions at times, but it did keep everything interesting.

We had orientation meetings in Miami and then again in Managua. There were a few problems to be ironed out; for example, someone had told the Nicaraguans we would be bringing tools. These problems were dealt with upon arriving, and the brigade was split into three groups. Mine worked around Managua for a month. The other folks went up north, some as far as Somoto near the Honduran border, where they had a chance to view the jeep that Marvin José Lopez was driving the last morning on his way to work. Others were trucked into the mountains outside of León, where eighteen of them shared quarters in a single room without running water in an isolated work camp.

Wood is still the main fuel source in the country, so large areas around the cities have been denuded of trees. The first site we worked at was Asososca lagoon, one of many water-filled volcanic craters. Nestled in steep slopes overlooking the city, the lagoon is the capital's main water supply. Last year, the water level fell a meter, causing government officials to be concerned about possible shortages in the future. In addition, a local farmer burned the foliage off the slopes above the lagoon, which is the cheapest way to clear the ground, and plowed a large field. He sprayed the field with herbicides and pesticides, and planted sorghum, which was coming up as we began working there. Since the farmer, like all Nicaraguan citizens, has the right to use government lands, the government was negotiating with him to get him to leave. Meanwhile, our reforestation efforts were aimed at preventing run-off and erosion of chemicals and topsoil into the lagoon, as well as improving the watershed quality of the soil around the reservoir.

The slopes were fairly steep, but previous crews of IRENA workers had done much of the heavier work of clearing with machetes already. We got trucked up to the site at about 7 AM and began hauling trees downhill and planting them by hand. We arranged for some shovels a week or two later. We only worked half days, since on sunny days the leaves of broadleafed little plants, like the oaks we were planting, would turn black. The heat was something some of the people from the midwest weren't used to, so we carried a lot of water, laced with drops of iodine by the prudent.

Six days a week we went out to work, after breakfasting at a "comedor popular" (employees' eatery) on the highway. They mainly served gallo pinto, the Nicaraguan national dish of rice and beans, along with some kind of meat and tortillas. Our health responsable, a nurse from Minneapolis, joked one morning that someone had put frog eggs into her drink. Some of the fruit beverages did look a bit exotic, pale pink or bright crimson, but I found them delicious and always seemed to be thinking about them late in the morning when the sun had been out on us for a couple of hours.

We were fortunate to be able to go into the capital every day after work, leaping into the jam-packed "Tipitapa" bus line, sometimes hanging onto the back of the vehicle all the way into town. The city buses were always something of an adventure; if anything, it forced you to use whatever Spanish you might have in finding out how to get from one place to the next. We saw tourist sites, famous spots, museums, restaurants, and marketplaces. We met North Americans, Nicaraguans, government workers, students, reporters. Once, while going through a tiny town in the back of a truck, a man pointed to us and said, "Sovieticos." But we never saw any, only some Russian tractors—which were brought in to replace acres of American vehicles rotting for lack of parts. We talked to everyone we could, watched the opposition parties on TV during their election campaigns, and read the papers, sharing the news with those of us who couldn't speak Spanish. *La Prensa,* the opposition paper, printed cartoons against us, portraying us as cavemen who might somehow drag Nicaragua into the stone age. Perhaps that's what they think of conservation. They printed another cartoon against internationalists in general, showing an almost empty bus of enthusiastic foreigners passing by a bus stop full of Nicaraguans. Articles about us appeared in the two popular papers, and we were interviewed on radio and television. We met with members of opposition parties, mass organizations, trade unions, government agencies, and the Sandinista National Liberation Front.

Nicaragua is so poor in industrial development it makes Mexico seem like a rich country. Unlike Mexico, however, there are no destitute Indian women begging in the streets with their malnourished children. The Nicaraguan people, however poor, are busy and working. Jovial young soldiers guarding the telephone exchange; quiet girls serving cokes at refreshment stands; kids walking home in their school uniforms; wrinkled, worn-out market stall women grinning at my sloppy Spanish; taxi drivers rushing through the dusty late afternoon traffic; people pursuing their lives— with dignity. There seemed to be little of the desperation (or its obverse, complacency) or the cynicism so prevalent in the U.S.

In Nicaragua life will continue to be hard, in peace and in war for some time to come. The barrios of Managua stretch out from the central district in rows of little shacks on muddy (or dusty, given the season) roads, some without electricity or running water. Vaqueros can be seen herding cattle through the vacant lots of downtown Managua. Horses graze on grass growing up through the broken pavement of a busy intersection. Children play in filthy drainage ditches, while a woman sweeps out the dirt floor of her shanty. Naked brown toddlers chase a duck through mud puddles in the rain. Kitchen workers adjusted their menu at the requests of the North American vegetarians.

Even the drunks we stopped for directions happened to be warmly gentle and generous. I realized these people were all the reason why their sons and brothers head for the war fronts with the slogan, "Luchamos para vencer!" We fight to win!

Sesshu Foster

Barrio Riguero Mass
(Iglesia Santa María de Los Angeles)
Managua 1984

The mural
the bleeding boat of Christ
flows, part of the
river here,
Christ's bloody hands
above the guitar
above the bombo
pulsing
throughout the church.
And the Chileans sing:
"Brothers and sisters
you have the power
in your hands."
As dark as mud
the man
who passes out
the chairs.

And the children
running in from
the muddy street,
here
most of them
wear shoes.
The woman in green
leans through the door,
her white teeth
at the young man's
ear...Her smile bright
in Nicaraguan green—
in militia green—
as the Chilean star
in the internationalists' eyes.

Sesshu Foster

Distant September

the volcanic slopes alive
with your firm tenderness
even as the walking sticks
and jumping spiders

and the disturbed ground
—by construction or
planting—under the last
standing water of the rainy season

Religious service in Iglesia Santa María de Los Angeles, Barrio Riguero, Managua, Nicaragua. Photo by Victor Sanchez.

grow shoots of bright grass,
and you go on working
where you are.

the faces in Managua pass
la Malinche in a crowded bus,
her girls pushing a cart

Marvin José Lopez Reforestation Brigade / 103

through the muddy street
smelling of rotting garbage,
past the Mercado Oriental,
or waiting for the bus in militia green.
I look for your face there,
or Marina's face in the child's
face: their eyes simply innocent
and dark

Do your days
pass like other days?
Like the clouds over Oaxaca
valley, amid a humble, working
people?
I string the mosquito net
between two rocking chairs
and sleep on the floor:
thunder storms at night and
dry lightning over Lake Managua.
(In the morning at the training
compound under the large trees
behind us, they begin the day
with Nueva Trova, as the big
trucks cross the Calle Pedro Joaquin
Chamorro—the northern highway—
pulling out of the zona franca,
formerly a somocista factory
now a prison,
for the fields.)
Later, in the fields myself, Danilo
hands me the cracked shovel
saying, "Made in Nicaragua.
It's shit." Meaning the legacy
of underdevelopment, and it's true:
the shovel widens a couple blisters
across my palm and then snaps
apart, while the planters put in

the trees behind me; my back bent
under that beautiful sky as
the sun comes out onto our skin
like a laying on of hands
light through the big cumulus,
light through the green leaves
as the creaking shovel turns out
moist sandstone and real dark earth.

After work, riding through the capital
in the back of a truck,
watching for you.

CONSTRUCTION BRIGADE
"Construyendo Por La Paz"
November 1984

Maestro Umberto, Nicaraguan responsable at the Construction Brigade work-site in barrio Edgard Munguía. Photo by Kevin Gerien.

Editor's Note—The Construction Brigade

More than most others, the Construction Brigade was made up of people active in the U.S. in support of the Nicaraguan Revolution. The organizers were seeking to leave a permanent example of North American solidarity. Through meetings with Nicaraguan representatives, they arranged to build a community center in the barrio Edgard Munguía and to work on a government construction project, building a school in barrio Bello Amanecer (Beautiful Dawn).

Joe Richey

Arriving in Bello Amanecer, children everywhere. Dusty barrio flanked by sorghum field and sugarcane. Looking down each street, the constant crisscrossing of kids and pigs and dogs and chickens. The sun is bright and hard. It is pounding down on us. This *is* the Third World, and all it seems to want is a ball to play with. Hundreds of children...Manuels, Miguels, Gustavos, Josés, Felipes, Enriques, Carlos, and one fair skinned boy, Jeffrey, whom all the other Nica boys push toward me.

FSLN campaign march through the barrio at night. Gathered at each intersection around a burning tire, lit firecrackers, chanted slogans, and sang the Sandinista anthem at attention and at least loud enough for any local reactionaries to hear.

All in all, barrio Bello Amanecer is FSLN territory, as is most everywhere I have seen so far. The other political parties just do not have their organizations together, nor have they done anything for the people.

Elaine Myrianthopoulos

Dear Friends:

Just a few quick words—I'm having the best *time*. When we touched down in Managua, every anxiety I'd ever had about this trip disappeared. The fact that we all made both planes, they were on time, all our luggage and crate upon crate upon crate of tools and hardware made the transfer in Miami and got here; all this is miraculous and has to be a good omen.

The people in the barrio are wonderful—enthusiastic about our being here, warm, generous beyond their means, patient, and militant. I'm staying with a woman who is a mother of heroes and martyrs. The CDS is our sponsor group and we marched with the barrio and 300,000 Managuans in the big FSLN rally yesterday. The work is really hard, but I'm learning many skills, and a lot about construction. *Everything* is by hand. We spent the first two days clearing the site, moving concrete slabs from another project, and shoveling gravel. Then the digging began—so it's been the physically hardest work first. When I'm not working, I can usually be found sleeping. Lot's of people from the barrio have been working with us, and there are kids *everywhere*. It's been really hard to use the polaroid,

Elaine Myrianthopoulos and Kermit Beauchamp mixing mortar in Managua. Photo by Kevin Gerien.

because as soon as they see it, I'm surrounded by thirty kids each wanting a picture.

All day long our work is interrupted by people bringing us little cakes, refrescos, cereal drinks, juice, and you just can't say no. Any thought of controlling what I eat so I won't get sick is hopeless. Our food is prepared by one of the women here, and the back yard area where she prepares it is like everyone else's—dirty, smoky, buggy. I don't mind it at all. These people are so incredibly generous and supportive and proud to have us here that I just take whatever they give me.

This whole barrio is a lesson in the benefits of the revolution. New houses going up in place of the shacks where people had been living, rent charged according to income. The kids are barefoot and dressed in rags, but they are all healthy, which continually amazes me, and they go to school (when they're not helping us on the site). The kids love to push wheelbarrows for us, which is a real help when we're digging dirt or gravel. They dump them and bring them back empty for us and then clown around until they're full again.

Sunday is the election, which will be very exciting, and I think Monday is going to be a big day of celebration.

So much for a few quick words! I miss you all.

Gwendolyn Gilliam

I went with América, Sonia's daughter, as she voted today. A teenager with hypnotic eyes, she was the first in her family to join the militia. When she finished, she pressed her red thumb, dipped in dye as a sign she had voted, against mine so I could share the redness. I heard that the soldiers in Estelí were using their thumbs to put kiss marks on each other's cheeks. Everyone was relieved that there were only a couple of isolated contra attacks at voting places across the country.

Editor's Note—Statement by the Construction Brigade

On November 6, 1984, election day in the United States, the members of the Construction Brigade went to the U.S. embassy in Managua to deliver the following message:

Young woman from León shows off her thumb dipped in red paint, indicating she has voted in Nicaraguan elections, November 4, 1984. Photo by Anthony Yarus.

We are the Nicaragua Construction Brigade: thirty North Americans who have come to Nicaragua to build.

Our government sends bombs; we deliver hammers and nails. Our government finances destruction and murder; we have traveled 3,000 miles to help Nicaraguans put their country back together.

We come out of a passionate conviction that our government is doing wrong and that, when a government does wrong, the people must speak for themselves.

We protest Ronald Reagan's undeclared war on Nicaragua: the millions of dollars of CIA aid to the contras (financing weapons and training that has resulted in useless death and destruction); the cruel economic sanctions against a country in desperate need of help; the gross violations of international law, such as the mining of the harbors.

The Sandinistas have done more for their people in five years than Somoza did in half a century. In place of death squads, torture chambers and unbridled corruption, they have instituted health care, education, and democracy—for all the people.

On this day of presidential elections in our country, we declare our determination to fight Ronald Reagan's immoral policies for as long as he—or any other president—persists in them.

We demand an end to the North American war against our friends, the people of Nicaragua, and we remind the world that the government of the United States does not necessarily speak for its citizens.

North Americans protest U.S. policies toward Nicaragua outside the U.S. Embassy, Managua, Nicaragua. Photo by Paul Tick.

Joan Harmon

Tonight is a terrible and depressing night. Reagan has won. Everyone here expects to die, and I dread returning to my country. I still don't know what it feels like to expect to die, but I don't think I can go back to New York without something having been drastically changed in me. Some went to the U.S. embassy today to make a statement, but I couldn't stand the thought of being in the same room with the men who can calmly and coldbloodedly justify the murder of these people. The moon is full tonight, and the dogs are barking and the lady in my house can't sleep because her son is at the front. It is all so terrible.

We who stayed here today, however, worked hard and well. We put six posts in for the school. It is starting to take shape and feels excellent to work your body hard in the melting sun. No matter how helpless you feel you have to keep on working. These people are the greatest inspiration I have ever had. Never have I seen such quiet, gentle strength.

Barrio Edgard Munguía, site of community center built by members of the Construction Brigade, November, 1984. Photo by Kevin Gerien.

Gwendolyn Gilliam

The day after Reagan's landslide victory and three days after the Nicaraguan presidential elections, a U.S. spy plane cracked the sound barrier over Managua. The boom it made had a weird shimmy, spreading like batter on a griddle. The Nicaraguans call the plane the black bird. The national anxiety level stepped up as it kept passing over, once a day for three days, and then three times on the fourth day. I know one old grandmother who never set her Bible down for four days.

On November 7, U.S. warships off both coasts pulled to within twelve miles off shore, and everyone thought the invasion was on. Tanks rumbled through the streets of Managua at 3:00 AM. After that they were parked in empty lots, with kids in and out of uniform hanging out on them.

On the second day of the sonic booms, I woke up to hear my first Voice of America broadcast from Costa Rica. They always call for the "liberation" of Nicaragua. Walking back to breakfast from the construction site, I noticed six parachutes swinging down about a mile ahead. It took me awhile to realize that they were Nicaraguans. If it was the invasion, there would have been many more. That night there were some new young men hanging out on the corner who turned out to be the paratroopers.

I met Jorge Gonzales Luna, who had been sitting in a cinema in Corinto when the CIA exploded four oil tanks. Jorge had packed up his truck with as many children as he could and evacuated them into the surrounding mountains, making fifteen trips in all. The oil tanks burned for four days, turning everything black.

Another time Jorge was delivering a truckload of shrimp to the army when the contras caught him and confiscated the shrimp. Before they could carry it off, the

Sandinistas attacked. Jorge dived into a ditch where he lay for the three days that the battle lasted. All the while he could smell the shrimp, which had cost him 1,250 dollars, rotting in the heat.

Joe Richey

This is no longer just a good-will mission.

We are in a state of war. The invasion appears imminent. My sense of hearing has heightened in geometric progressions of paranoia after Daniel Ortega's emergency speech calling Nicaraguans to defend the capital; that sense of history happening, the rumblings of a nation mobilizing, and how eerie for little Arelelias to be fast asleep while the adults talk strategies. Seeing her curled up, her mouth slightly open, her small eyelids and limp fingers, that innocence. I imagined the mushroom cloud's shadow sweeping over her and the whole room lighting up.

Couldn't sleep.

Roosters crowing a block away became human screams. Dogs were barking at enemy troops creeping through the sorghum field. Foreign bird calls became contra commanders calling out orders in code. I hear helicopters in every breeze, not to mention Ronaldo starting his motorcycle at 5 AM.

Couldn't take what my fatalistic bedtime imagination was doing any longer, so I got some pants on and opened the door. New Morning. Like when the "Wizard of Oz" turns to a color film. A new world, alive and sure of itself getting ready for work. Dogs walked the streets, chickens pecking around in the dirt, sun not yet in the sky, that pastel shade of light.

I walked down to the construction site, waved to the lonely guard who watches the equipment in the school, and sat down to photograph the bello amanecer shining through the concrete columns we've been setting in place.

no MIGs here
just a humming bird
sipping nectar after the rain....

Jim Calder

Too many crossroads headed in the same direction. November 8—my wife in Nicaragua, MIGs on a bogus boat ride, Reagan on a landslide, and Veterans Day celebrating a new statue and strategy.

Vietnam veterans were expected to show up in great numbers to view the newest statue that is to give honor to the fighting men of the era by physicalizing the shape of a few GIs. I felt frightened to the bone of a monstrous juggernaut that spews fire and words in many directions but is constantly headed one way. I thought to myself, "They could kill my wife and just make a cover story about it." I took the next train to Washington.

Joan Harmon

The roosters are at it now, and people are sending the children out for food. We are consumed by the relentless barking of dogs in the night. And always the banging on doors as people are awakened for revolutionary vigilance.

The moon is flattening out like a soccer ball losing air. Each night seems more charged than the last. An old battered stationwagon pulls up with three soldiers in it. I am still amazed how there is never any fear of the police. The banana trees and the FSLN banners are rustling in a night wind. Indeed this is charged soil, sacred, as Cardenal has said, a giant tomb because of the blood shed upon it.

Yesterday the tanks went by in the morning going into Managua, a half-hour long parade. The neighborhood people began working on their bomb shelters—digging under the moon and a 100 watt bulb—laughing and joking as they do. Such joyousness, music, and dancing in the face of preparing for war.

We are all thinking to ourselves, what if Reagan makes it impossible for North Americans to come here while they proceed to murder the Nicaraguans? How will it feel to have our hands tied as we imagine which one of these children has been blown up today?

Andrew Courtney,
Joan Harmon,
Elaine Myrianthopoulos

Describe the community center that you built.

AC: It is a nice big space; it has a seismic beam foundation to protect it from the earthquakes and tremors that are common in Nicaragua. We built a beautiful woodwork exterior. As an innovation, we built large sliding doors, the kind of thing you might see in New Hampshire, that open up onto a large vista of the city of Managua. It's not quite finished. It doesn't have a roof because roofing is in great shortage. It soon will. It will become a health clinic and day-care facility, with a little library for the neighborhood. It will have an office for the local CDS and is large enough for community meetings. It's a beautiful structure.

You mentioned shortages.
What was in short supply when you were there?

AC: Shortages run from not having enough toilet paper to a shortage of nails. Nicaragua is not an industrial society, nor has it ever been. In order to make toilet paper, you have to have a paper industry. Under Somoza, Nicaragua lived off its parasitic relationship with the United States. Where does Nicaragua get supplies from now that the U.S. has cut off so much of its trade? From the construction point of view, you have to have an industry that makes roofing. It doesn't just magically appear. You have to have an industry that makes nails. When we arrived in the barrio, we found people using homemade hammers. We brought down Black and Decker power tools. In order to use them, we had to extend power lines to the work site.

Construction brigadistas at work on the framing for the community center, barrio Edgard Munguía. Photo by Kevin Gerien.

JH: I found a wide range of reactions to the shortages. One woman, Victoria, who cooked for us and is the local head of the CDS, said she would be willing to eat leaves just for the country to be left alone. Other people are just angry that they can't get things or that things at the store are expensive. There is a distribution system that sees that people get enough basics: rice, beans, cooking oil. We did not see anyone going hungry in either barrio during the month we were there.

Who were the Nicaraguans who worked with you on the projects? Who did you live with?

JH: In Bello Amanecer, our boss was a construction worker who works independently part-time and sometimes with the CDS. It was his job to organize the brigade and to be our foreman. Other than that, there were volunteers from the neighborhood. People would help whenever they could.

AC: In barrio Edgard Munguía, there were at least four men and many many children all the time working with us.

EM: I lived with a woman named Mercedes who had lost a son in the Revolution. He was nineteen when he died in 1974. She was a staunch Sandinista. She often talked about how her life had changed since the Revolution. She had several grown-up children and also some very tiny kids. When we asked her about the little ones, she told us that Nicaraguans had been asked to raise production, and this was how she had done it. She sewed for a living. I never saw anyone work as hard as she and her kids.

There was a woman who used to come by every night after work named Pastora. She worked in the office of the Sandinista youth. She was very lively and full of fun, and she became a great friend. We would talk and ask her questions. We could ask her anything. She brought some of the Sandinista youth by to talk with us. She had three little kids who would come and play in the house. Two days before I left she said to me: "Well, I've been mobilized." I said "What does that mean?" She said, "I'm mobilized for defense for three months." I asked her where she was going and if she was afraid. She said she wasn't afraid and would go wherever she was sent. To me she represented the spirit and enthusiasm of the people in this barrio. The last day I learned that she was being sent to Jinotega, an area of strong contra activity. Her kids went to live with her mother. I often wonder how she is doing.

When you went back for the inauguration, what had changed since last November? Had the mood of the country changed?

AC: I went back last week to attend the inauguration (January 10, 1985) and to evaluate the work on our two project sites. I noticed that an entirely new barrio had been built across the street from barrio Edgard Munguía. In the ten days that I just spent in Nicaragua, that barrio went from 50 homes to 100 homes. Another new barrio was going up just south of Edgard Munguía.

I see this as some kind of growth optimism, coming at the same time as Nicaragua is getting their new President, Daniel Ortega, and their new Vice-President, Sergio Ramirez. We were there, watching as they assumed their offices. And of course, in walks Fidel Castro, a big tall man. His beard is getting more salt-and-peppery. He sat down and listened attentively to Ortega's speech.

Nicaraguan presidential candidate Daniel Ortega visits "Habitat for Humanity" worksite on New York City's Lower East Side, October, 1984. Photo by Anthony Yarus.

That evening there was a grand, festive celebration in the park next to the Plaza de la Revolución, with lots of dancing and carrying on. It's a popular relation to the new government, and the people just flowed into that park. They rejoiced and we joined with them.

Revolution is a mother. Sometimes pretty, sometimes not. But you cannot reject her because she is yours. Revolution is very long, very hard. It is never done for the present generation, but for the children who will grow into it. If you look at Revolution as for yourself, you would never endure the hardships. It is a very sweet and sour thing.

Marcos Gonzalez,
Secretary for International
Relations of the Union of Small
Growers and Ranchers

HARVEST BRIGADES
November 1984–March 1985

Harriet Tubman Brigade, November 28–December 19, 1984
harvested coffee near Matagalpa

Jean Donovan Brigade, December 18, 1984–January 7, 1985
harvested coffee near Matagalpa

Los Semilleros, January 4–February 1, 1985
harvested coffee near Matagalpa

Heroes and Martyrs of Tel Cor, January 8–30, 1985
harvested coffee in El Crucero (includes
Elders Brigade)

Los Adoquines, February 1–27, 1985
harvested coffee in El Crucero (includes
Veterans Brigade)

Fannie Lou Hamer Brigade, February 10–25, 1985
harvested cotton near León

Sandy Pollack Peace Brigade, February 19–March 4, 1985
harvested cotton near León

At work the Latinos lead the chants. They are from Argentina and Venezuela, Bolivia, Guatemala and Mexico, and they chant: "Here, there, the Yanqui Will Die!" The pain in my heart grows. The Nicaraguans ask them not to sing this around us. They say we are not Yanquis. That we who have come to help are all of one heart, which is the heart of freedom. They say that we, also, are Nicaraguans.

Janet Essley,
Brigadista

I'll never lose my ties with the United States. I'm not a foreigner when I'm in the United States, and I don't refer to the United States from an outsider's point of view. The United States will always be a part of me, and, in my heart, I'll always be a part of the United States.

Anastasio Somoza Debayle,
Former Dictator

Editor's Note—Harvest Brigades

Harvest brigades continued during the 1984–1985 season, this time organized by staff members of the *Brigadista Bulletin* who had been working on program evaluation and follow-up organizing of the previous year's brigades. As the Nicaragua Exchange, they began to train brigade leaders and health workers, work with local organizers, and recruit brigadistas. Nicaragua asked for seven North American brigades, for varying work periods of two to four weeks, to help meet the severe shortage caused by the emergency fall mobilization of more than 30,000 Nicaraguan students for defense. Despite the escalation of the war, and the increased risks of working in a country under siege, nearly 400 new brigadistas volunteered; among them an "elders squad" of people over sixty-five and a group of U.S. veterans.

Zachary Sklar

Coffee, which brought in 150 million dollars in export revenues last year, is Nicaragua's principal source of foreign exchange. It is no coincidence, therefore, that in 1984, the contras destroyed eighty state-owned and a dozen private coffee farms in the departments of Matagalpa and Jinotega,

This story includes excerpts from "Bringing the War Home in Nicaragua: Report from the Coffee Fields" by Zachary Sklar, *The Nation*, 240 (5), February 9, 1985. Reprinted with permission.

where 75 percent of the crop is grown. Most U.S. journalists are based in Managua, away from the fighting, and have focused on issues like Arturo Cruz's role in the elections, press censorship, draft resistance, shortages, grumblings about Sandinista inefficiency. What they have failed to convey to the U.S. public is the single most important fact about Nicaragua today: it is engaged in a full-scale war.

Seventeen of us, calling ourselves the Harriet Tubman brigade, joined with volunteers from seventeen other countries, organized as the Maurice Bishop International Brigade. Ranging in age from twelve to seventy-four, we were the first of thousands, including 500 more from the United States, who have gone to Nicaragua to pick coffee and cotton this winter. We worked at two farms, San José and La Lima, located in a relatively secure area of the war zone, just north of the city of Matagalpa.

Before the contra war, seventy-five permanent residents lived at San José. By the time we arrived, twenty-three young men from the farm were serving in the army, and the 300 migrant laborers who usually help with the harvest had been transferred farther north to pick in the more dangerous border areas. The farm's production quota has been reduced to 1,000 quintals (about 10,000 pounds) of export-grade coffee beans. Three years ago, San José's workers harvested 1,700 quintals.

At night, we occasionally heard gunfire and saw red tracers arching like fireworks through the black sky. Still, the protected setting made us feel remote from physical danger, until one day when the news crackled over short-wave radio that a volunteer brigade of twenty-one TelCor (telephone and postal) workers on their way to pick coffee had been ambushed north of Estelí. The contras had blown up their bus with mortar fire, hacked the few survivors to death with machetes, and set their bodies on fire.

That night our brigade joined hands with the people of San José and sang a hymn for the murdered workers. The memorial service was held in San José's wooden one-room schoolhouse, which is named for a local hero, Salvador Gonzalez, a teacher whose framed photograph hangs on the wall. In three years, he taught all but five of the previously illiterate residents of San José to read and write. Like the TelCor workers, Salvador Gonzalez was killed by the contras. When he died, on January 19, 1984, he was twenty-two years old. He left two small daughters, who are now counted among the approximately 500 war orphans in the region.

As our skills improved and good weather provided more time for picking, our sacks grew heavier. Workers from neighboring farms joined us, and the days passed quickly. But one afternoon near the end of our stay, I looked out at the endless rows of red spreading before me, and I understood for the first time just how shorthanded the war has left Nicaragua. Work as hard as we might, we would never come close to doing it all. About half of those juicy red beans were destined to turn black on the branches or shrivel and fall to the ground.

We easily forget that many of Nicaragua's problems, big and small, are the direct result of the contra war. Just how easily, I realized on the day we left for home. The farm's truck dropped us in the city of Matagalpa, where another truck was to have met us. But it was nowhere to be found. For eight hours we waited as UNAG officials searched for some means of transportation to get us back to Managua. Bored and irritated, some of us complained, just as Nicaraguans do, about the bumbling bureaucracy.

When a truck finally arrived, we heard the explanation for the delay. That morning the contras had burned down seven private haciendas and one coffee storage plant to the north, near Yalí. As a last reminder of the pervasiveness of the war, the truck scheduled for us had been commandeered to help transport the eight dead and seven wounded.

Nicaragua is so poor. The people have so little. But what they have is tremendous: a sense that Nicaragua is their own, that they can make of it what they want, that there is hope, that their views and complaints will be heard and understood. There is a nobility to the struggle, an honoring of all who have contributed, a memory and reverence for those who have died, a willingness to die defending something that you've suffered to win and that will be better for your children. It is a society of the future.

It was inspiring and thrilling to be in a country where socialism is not a dirty word, where people share my values, where they reach out to include rather than push people out. It gives me strength and pushes me out of my own personal problems and depressions. I feel liberated and energetic from having risked and struggled and survived and done my part.

Audrey Seniors

In June 1984, I made my first visit to Nicaragua, meeting with the Mothers of Heroes and Martyrs, a group of mothers whose children had been killed in the fight against Somoza or by the contras. A statement made by a mother whose daughter had been killed by the contras stands out in my mind. She asked us to tell the mothers in the United States not to let their sons come to invade Nicaragua: "We know what it is like to lose a child and we do not wish it to happen to anyone else. But if your sons come here to invade us, they will be killed."

Many times since I have reflected on these words and what they mean for Black and Latino mothers and families here. History has shown, in Vietnam and most recently in Grenada, that it is Blacks and the poor who are on the front line fighting the United States' dirty wars. Black mothers must bury our sons, and all of us suffer the emotional and economic hardship of their loss to our communities.

The Reagan administration has spent over 100 million dollars in its attempt to overthrow the Nicaraguan government. It is lobbying for 14 million dollars more for this year alone. At the same time, in Black communities across the country, we have been faced with tremendous cutbacks: in health care, day care, education, food stamps, grants to higher education. Our teenagers have the highest unemployment rate in the nation. Our rate of infant mortality has risen to almost twice the rate of white infants since Reagan started cutting social programs.

On December 18, 1984, I returned to Nicaragua for the second time, one of a group of seventy-four North Americans going to work in the coffee fields. To show my support for the Nicaraguan people and the revolution, as well as my opposition to the Reagan administration's support of the contras, I was to spend three weeks in Nicaragua cutting coffee.

In the Miami airport, I sat looking around at what was to become the Jean Donovan Brigade, named after one of the church women who was killed in El Salvador by a right-wing death squad in 1980. Anxious to return, I wondered what it would be like living and working with so many different people from so many different parts of North America.

The week before, someone had attempted to snatch my bag off my shoulder, and someone else had robbed my daughter's apartment. I looked forward to three weeks of feeling safe and secure, even though I knew I would be in a country at war.

After two and a half days of orientation in Managua, we boarded buses and began a seven hour trip to Matagalpa in the North. As we traveled into the mountains and beautiful countryside, passing through the picturesque city of Matagalpa, night began to overtake us. I thought of the murders of the TelCor (telecommunications) workers, who were on their way to cut coffee, of the mothers who were murdered on the way to visit their sons and daughters at the front. I also thought of the brothers and sisters in Southern Africa; the young, the old, murdered, dying, and suffering there. I thought of the atrocities carried out in Third World countries, supported with weapons and monies supplied by the United States government.

Finally, we reached our destination. As we climbed off the trucks we were greeted with applause, songs, and chants. What a welcome from the people of La Lima. There were speeches of greeting, revolutionary songs and chants, and tears in my eyes.

La Lima is a coffee farm that was once privately owned. The owner had allowed the coffee fields to grow wild, the hacienda and the land around it to deteriorate from years of neglect. Within the last year the government has taken control, the workers and families have begun rebuilding the farm and its coffee fields, now theirs.

To reach La Lima's coffee fields, you have to climb the mountains. The highest places I had ever climbed previously were the subway stairs of New York. I was determined to climb those mountains and either to lose my fear of heights or at best ignore it.

Each morning we were awakened at 4 AM to wash, dress, breakfast, and leave for the fields by 6 AM. We were summoned to line up by the sound of a large sea shell being blown. There were approximately 130 brigadistas from Argentina, Australia, Colombia, Guatemala, Ecuador, France, Spain, and North America. We were told then who were the top cutters of the previous day, what today's production goals were, and where we would be cutting. We were led to the fields by Nicaraguan workers and some militia people for our protection.

At noon we returned from the fields for lunch, all starving. By 12:30 we were on our way back to finish the day's cutting. Between 4 and 4:30 PM we returned again, with our coffee sacks on our shoulders, ready for weigh-in. We were happy, tired, wet, and muddy. Even though the rainy season was supposedly over, someone forgot to tell Mother Nature—it rained every day.

We celebrated Christmas eve with the other internationalists and the families of La Lima. We prepared gifts and made a piñata for the children. The foreman slaughtered a cow for the holiday meal.

Before returning to Managua, we made a stop at one of the coffee plants to see how the coffee was processed. Later we were told that our brigade had surpassed the amount of coffee the Nicaraguans had predicted we would cut. That made us happy, and that happiness was the hope that we were of some help to the people and the economy of Nicaragua.

Nicaragua is a beautiful country: the lushness of the countryside is a wonder. The people are friendly, pleasant, and helpful. The Nicaraguans should have the right to determine their own future without interference from the United States. My experience cutting coffee was a good one—and my stay away from Nicaragua will be a short one.

Lois Wessel

In Matagalpa it rained every day. We weren't prepared for it. People got sick, and it was bad for morale. Juan Pablo Villagra was in charge of the empresa in the area, which included thirty-three coffee UPEs and several cattle farms. He had been a fighter in the mountains. He told us how much the campesinos in Matagalpa loved the coffee trees.

He told us how much the trees give to the people. He told us how to treat the trees: never pull down the branches; don't pick the green beans, pick the red ones, one at a time; don't pick the stems because that's where next year's beans will grow. When we got to El Crucero, we worked with a brigade of teachers from the Ministry of Education. They were city folk like us, not campesinos. They were only interested in picking as much coffee as possible. They treated the trees badly. I cringed remembering what Juan Pablo told us.

At a meeting, someone asked Juan Pablo about his life during the revolution. He said that his real work began after the 19th of July, 1979, because that's when they had to rebuild and recreate the society. That struggle was much harder and more important than his time in the mountains fighting, he said. He urged us to live with the agricultural workers and consume all of their reality. He made a point of calling them workers, not peasants.

I think that most of the political experience you get on the brigades comes from conversations with the campesinos. Something will strike you from a conversation in the kitchen, something will happen by the side of the road. North Americans tend to want to know facts, about the literacy campaign, about vaccinations. I feel that people who want to know facts and figures can find them in the States because so much is published. Many of the Nicaraguans themselves don't know these numbers. What you can't get from books is the experience of working in the fields, personal contacts, the chance to speak Spanish.

There are a lot of banana trees in the coffee fields. They help provide shade. In the old days, the workers weren't allowed to pick the bananas. If they did, it would have to be at night. They would hide the bananas in the houses. In the morning the National Guard would come and look. If they had any fruit in their homes, they would be denied a day's pay. They had to buy all their food at the company store. The prices were always set at more than the people had.

The Guard would be standing at the door. You couldn't disagree with the price.

There used to be a lot of Honduran and Salvadoran migrant workers who came to work in the harvest. Now their governments won't let them in. And there's a lot of land that has been given over to agrarian cooperatives as part of the land reform program. There is such a labor shortage that they've closed the Ministry of Culture for three weeks to help bring in the coffee. There were seventy-five of us in Matagalpa. There was also a brigade of Norwegians, a brigade of Spanish, and a group of people called Internacionalistas, foreigners who live and work in Managua. They included Argentinians, Mexicans, Guatemalans, Venezuelans, a Swiss woman, and a man from France.

Coffee is measured differently in different parts of the country. In Matagalpa the unit of measure is called a lata. Lata means can. You pour the coffee from your bag into a large can. It's a volume measurement. Then you have a lata y media, literally a can and a half. Cuartillo means a quarter. A little left over is called polvo, which means dust. For example, you could pick two lata's y polvo, which means two cans plus dust. Working with the Argentinians was funny. In Argentina, polvo means ejaculation. Every time one of them got a measurement like dos latas y polvo, they just laughed and laughed.

One night Liz and Penny brought me over to translate because they were so excited to see a female with a gun (that's how they approached me—"Come translate please, there's a woman with a gun!!"). Norma, twenty years old and wearing a T-shirt that said "sigame...voy con el frente" (Follow me, I go with the Frente Sandinista) from the recent elections, was sitting there smiling next to a guy that looked equally young. He turned out to be her husband. They had two sons.

We talked to her for several hours about her life as a woman in the revolution and in the new society. After she was talked out, her husband, who had been quiet the whole time, said: "Hey, look…you asked her all about women and the revolution, but can I say something? Before the revolution we all thought that women weren't worth anything. We were told this. Now we know that men and women are equal, and sure this idea has helped women. But it has also helped men. Men are better off because we have all gained."

I think it would be very difficult to return to Mexico, where I lived for a while. In the countryside in Mexico, they have accepted their destiny and feel powerless. Everything is "si Dios quiere" (if God wants it…).

There was a priest named Porfirio Pascual, a Spaniard, with the Spanish brigade in Matagalpa. He was in his late forties and an incredible coffee picker. He was usually the first one up and the first in line. He told me about his church in Zaragoza, Spain. He once rang the bell at 3 AM. People came running, saying "Father, father, what is the matter? Why are you ringing bells in the middle of the night?" He answered loudly, "NICARAGUA IS BEING INVADED!!" He recently wrote a letter to the Pope, inviting him to come to Nicaragua to pick coffee.

He gave a mass for Christmas eve. It was beautiful. Before the mass began, several of the Jewish brigadistas lit the Chanukah candles and said the blessings. All of the children gathered around and watched the candles start to drip. Porfirio then gave a talk about Joseph, Mary, and baby Jesus living and working in the country—just like us—and he compared their barn to the barn we were in. He asked for hope and liberation for those in El Salvador, Palestine, and South Africa. He talked about Reagan and Queen Elizabeth celebrating Christmas while others were suffering. He christened two babies, using a canteen belonging to one of the brigadistas. Just when he began singing songs at the end, the Chanukah candles went out.

Earl Christy

Everything in Matagalpa was a lot more primitive than in El Crucero. It was much more mountainous. There was no place to go. There was one store five kilometers away. And you couldn't be on the road at night.

One time we went to the neighboring UPE. There are many Salvadoran refugees in Nicaragua, and they had formed a coffee-picking brigade.

We spent a Sunday visiting with them. They put on a program for us that was really nice. Lots of talks, speeches, music. When we walked back that night we had about eight militia people with us. We had heard mortar fire that day and later learned that a tobacco farm in the southern department of Jinotega had been destroyed.

Our UPE was between two others: El Robar to the south, where the Salvadoran refugees were, and UPE San Antonio. San Antonio was attacked while we were there. We heard gun fire while we were picking. There were no casualties.

At the UPE where we worked, there were about 300 Miskitu Indians. They were refugees. Only two of them spoke English, only a few spoke Spanish. They were mostly from the area around the Río Coco in the department of Jinotega. Some were from the northeast, from Zelaya along the Atlantic.

They came to the UPE sometime in 1983. They had been caught in the middle of the war. Some of them had been given land titles. The government was building houses for them. Then the fighting got too intense in southern Jinotega, so they were moved again, into Matagalpa. The older people seemed to want to go back more than the younger people.

The majority blamed the U.S. for their troubles. "Why don't you all just leave us alone?" "What has Nicaragua done to you?" They couldn't understand why the U.S. was pushing the war.

When we got back to Managua, we learned of bigger contra attacks. Twelve people were killed and twelve children orphaned during one attack that occurred in Matagalpa while we were there. Contra attacks are increasing in Matagalpa. Before, they concentrated their attacks on the coffee harvest in Jinotega.

Janet Essley

The last day of picking coffee in Matagalpa the sun shines. The trees are loaded like Christmas with red, so we will remember always how romantic the coffee fields are and want to return next year. It is hard to imagine, sometimes, the alchemy through which the little red ones will become schools or clinics. And, sometimes, hard to remember those fighting in the mountains, without beds or food or the safety to talk without fear of ambush. These are hard to visualize, even though every morning, with the announcement of the previous day's vanguard pickers, Orlando or Chavelo or Federico remind us and thank us for our contribution, hoping that gratitude will increase our productivity. The campesinos listen respectfully to these speeches. They have endured through hunger and disease, the National Guard and insurrection, and now the war. I hope that this current demand for patience, as North Americans are praised for work they have always performed unpraised, amuses them.

Far below, the horn sounds the end of the work day, the call to measure our labor. I have five latas in my sack. Federico, measuring me out, is so encouraging. I do not have the heart to tell him that Sharon had used my sack when hers was full. Poor Federico. Responsible for brigades of Latinos, Europeans, and North Americans, he is exhausted from walking, simultaneously, several cultural tightropes.

On my fourth journey along the highway between Matagalpa and Managua, we stop for lunch in a town at a crossroads. Three busloads of us unload into the cafes. Louisa and Paul and I settle for a coke. We offer some hitchhiking soldiers a ride to Managua, thinking of all the stories they could tell us. They decline, lest their presence endanger us. We apologize silently. Once again we have forgotten the war.

Anne Rodman

From Evaluation of Health Program

Role of Responsable

The responsable did an excellent job keeping brigadistas healthy. Many also took care of Nicaraguan patients in areas where there was no local health worker. In some cases, the responsable made formal "rounds" in the morning to evaluate sick people. If there were many, or some who needed follow-up, the health responsable would stay in the barracks; otherwise she would go late to the fields. On brigades where there is only one health responsable, it is difficult to know whether she should stay back with the sickest people or go to the fields to be available for emergencies.

Hygiene

Self: lack of water and washing facilities made it difficult to wash as often as necessary. Wearing shoes reduced, but couldn't eliminate, contact with soil contaminated with human and animal waste. In rainy areas the brigadista is covered in mud, and in dry areas contaminated dust blows into everything. Convenient water would make it more likely that people would wash and probably reduce the number of infected cuts.

Recommendation: each group should have several large common water containers. A "water responsable" can be in charge of filling them and purifying the water for toothbrushing and drinking.

Food: healthy and boring.

Recommendation: bring spices, hot sauce, etc. Warn brigadistas to chew "lightly" because of the rocks in the rice and beans. Remind brigadistas that popsicles are made of impure water.

Environment: at most UPEs there is no system of garbage disposal since the campesinos don't have much to throw away.

First Aid

The most common first aid problems were minor cuts, stings of scorpions and insects, irritation from urticating caterpillars, and trauma from falls. Ant bites and chiggers were constant annoyances.

Recommendation: for polla—brigadistas who came in contact with the hairs of this urticating caterpillar experienced local pain and paresthesias, which persisted for a period of time varying from minutes to days, nausea, and sometimes dizziness. The local treatment is a "shot" and a "pink pill," one of which may be an antihistamine. Suggest cleaning the area to remove any hairs, and Tylenol.

Local Health System

Because of lack of transportation, the reluctance to travel at night, the lack of diagnostic facilities, and the lack of personnel trained to North American standards, brigadistas should be aware of the limitations of referral to the local clinic or hospital and the difficulty in many cases of a prompt referral. On one occasion when it was advisable to take a brigadista to the hospital in Matagalpa for evaluation, there was a delay in obtaining transportation because the closest radio was at a neighboring UPE. Once radio contact was made with the Empresa, it turned out there were no vehicles with headlights—in a complex of fifty farms. The risk of traveling at night in areas of possible contra activity has to be balanced against the potential benefit of evaluation and care at a local hospital. Although their help was not needed, it was good to know that brigadistas could be referred to the North American doctors working in Managua.
Recommendation: end the war.

Betty Bishop

Shortly before Christmas, a young coworker showed me a leaflet on the Elders Brigade. Until that moment I had assumed that at fifty-three I could not be helpful in doing hard physical work.

Before leaving for Nicaragua, we Elders had several meetings. At the first one I saw several familiar faces, including Sarah Crome, the organizer of the Elders Brigade. We pooled our knowledge on suitable clothes, accessories, and medication. The fact that we worked as a group prior to our departure gave us a solidarity that helped us to adjust both to the larger brigadista group and to Nicaragua.

I was most happy with the forty-two of us who went to UPE Carlos Espinoza. The age range, eighteen to seventy-eight, kept us flexible, humorous, and cooperative. The work was more difficult than I had anticipated. I found the weighing in at the end of the day demoralizing. It seemed to foster competition, which did not lead to as much productivity as pooling our bags and setting group goals might have. A few individuals rushed to the best parts of the best trees to chalk up a good weight at the end of the day. When we began weighing in, I again wondered about my suitability for the brigade. Was I worth the trouble it took to feed me? Would it have been more appropriate to be a Witness for Peace?

As our stay progressed, the hills we worked became steeper. Mimicking the campesinos, we began to carve ganchos, long sticks with a hook at the end, useful both in navigating steep terrain and in pulling down branches. The trick was to stand uphill from the tree and twist the branch down in such a way as to make the beans accessible without snapping a twig. Since there was a good deal of overgrowth, everyone did not spot the polla, a caterpillar that stings

Members of the Elders Brigade unfurl their banner at Sandino International Airport, January 8, 1985. Photo by Victoria Alba.

upon contact. Its sting is powerful enough to paralyze momentarily and incapacitate for as long as a day. The campesinos recommend rubbing the afflicted area with pol-la intestines, but I don't think any of us ever caught up with a polla.

Jaime Wheelock, Minister of Agriculture, visited us at the farm and invited us to join him at the end of our stay on a trip to the Matagalpa region. He wanted to show us a cooperative farm as well as the new giant sugar plant, so that we who had been living with the wounds of the past could glimpse the future. The sugar factory will be an automated, ecologically sound industry, employing 6,000 people, generating energy from alcohol, processing sugar, fabricating plastics, and growing and burning eucalyptus. The farm was a cooperative of diversified crops, with women and men economic equals and children well dressed, wearing shoes and attending school.

We then attended a meeting in the auditorium at Matagalpa hospital between Sandinista leaders and several private growers who were being kept from farming by the contras. We climaxed our day with dinner at the farm of Samuel Amador, a wealthy rice grower and member of the National Assembly. He sides with the Sandinistas because they are honest and is living testimony to the Sandinistas' commitment to a mixed economy.

Morris Wright

Only a few people of any generation are privileged to feel the elevation of spirit that accompanies release from tyranny and a collective forward motion to improve the human condition. We felt the excitement and uplift of such a surge—in the bubbling spirits of a youth brigade who joined us to pick coffee, in the rush of words and gestures by a farm worker telling of the changes in farm workers' lives from the degradation and misery of Somoza's time to the dignity and hope of his present life, in the huge throng at the inauguration of the newly elected government in Managua. This collective uplift of spirit is a precious thing, far too rare in this world. Two hundred years after our own revolution we are trying to *stamp out* a new spirit of fraternity and hope in Nicaragua.

What can a North American learn about a Central American country, its problems and its direction, while struggling to pick coffee on a steep mountainside, sleeping on a board, eating rice and beans, bathing from a bucket of cold water?

Sarah Crome, organizer of the Elders Brigade, picking coffee near El Crucero, January, 1985. Photo by Victoria Alba.

We learned very well what Nicaragua had been in 1979 at the time of the Sandinista revolution that overthrew the brutal dictator Anastasio Somoza. The farm where we worked was in a safe area, away from attacks by U.S.-supplied contras and so was not a priority area for attention by the new government. Physical conditions were much like those of Somoza's time. Human relations now are different: everyone is fairly paid for work; women are paid, not just the men; people are not beaten for eating fruit that grows among the coffee trees; the workers have a union.

The former owner fled to Miami six months after the revolution, but not until after he had set fire to the buildings where coffee had been processed. The charred remains of the buildings and machinery are a daily reminder of a regime that said, in effect, "If we can't exploit you any longer, then we'll harm you as much as we can." We could not escape the analogy between that act of sabotage and the present role of our government in backing the contras.

Janet Essley

The union is planning something special, so we must walk between two UPEs along the ridges of El Crucero. The walk is wonderful. In the distance, Managua looks tiny and fragile. The walk would be hard on the Elders, so the union has sent a truck. Someone wants a bench to keep clothing clean, so we have to raid the kitchen. As responsable, I go to explain to Soccorro, the cook, this latest group need. Her understanding is immense. Some people are geniuses of communication, so aware of the range of human thought and expression, that language is not an impediment to understanding. Soccorro is one of these. She is also a magician with a cauldron of rice, and possibly a saint. She waits each night to lock the kitchen only after we have satisfied ourselves with the electric light. Behind the exhaustion in her eyes, there is no resentment, nor envy in the wish that she could have clothing as warm as ours.

The human spirit is not grounded in the concept that each should possess the same material wealth. What is required is not equivalence of property, but equality in respect. Because those with the power of wealth never understand this, there will always be revolution.

John Strong

My interest in Nicaragua went back to the revolution of 1979 when the Sandinista Front wrested control of the country from the Somoza dictatorship. It was encouraging to see the country released from a stranglehold of poverty and exploitation. A year ago, after listening to some people who had been brigadistas and in the Witness for Peace program, I decided to volunteer to pick coffee. As a historian, I was attracted by the opportunity to actually take part in the making of history. On a personal level, there was the thrill of adventure. Another dimension was added when my daughter Lisa, a first year student at Mt. Holyoke, decided to come along.

Our arrival in Managua was highlighted by an unexpected welcome from Abbie Hoffman, who was leading a group of journalists and scholars through a tour of the country. After an enthusiastic greeting, Abbie removed his jacket to display a T-shirt with an anticontra message in Spanish. He stripped off the T-shirt and tossed it out as a gift to anyone who wanted it. The surprise visit of a figure from the sixties evoked a sense of nostalgia in those of us over forty and symbolized a historic continuity in U.S. political protest across a generation. This was lost on my daughter, who asked me who "that guy" was and why anyone would want his shirt.

Our fellow brigade members came from a diversity of backgrounds. The two largest were students and retired adults. Sarah Crome, the leader of the Elders contingent, had contacted all the people she could find who, as one of them put it, "had retired from jobs but not from life." The elders were an inspiration to us middle-aged brigadistas, who had doubts about being able to keep up with the students. The one who put us all to shame was a seventy-three year old retired laborer from Pennsylvania. Paul Glebovich picked coffee the same way he had lived—with enthusiasm and dedication. Once he got started on his row of coffee there was no stopping him. He seldom took a break for lunch! If you were fortunate enough to be picking next to him and if you could keep up with his pace, you would be rewarded with fascinating historical anecdotes about the development of labor unions in the Pennsylvania coal fields back in the days of John L. Lewis.

The campesinos in charge of our brigades, Mario and Zacharia, were experienced coffee workers, who knew which trees were ready for harvesting. They marched on ahead of us, clearing the way with formidable looking, razor sharp machetes. The first day out, one brigadista stepped into what she thought for one frightening moment was a nest of coral snakes. It had been one adult snake until the machete reduced it to fragments.

We walked along a narrow pathway between two ridges that rose sharply to a height of fifty or sixty feet above us.

At the top, the ridge leveled off for about twenty feet and then descended into another valley. I was reminded of Cortez's response to King Charles when asked to describe the nature of the terrain in Mexico. Cortez picked up a piece of paper, wadded it up, and tossed it down on the table. "That," he said, "is a perfect map of Mexico." The description fits the coffee hills of Nicaragua.

The nature of the landscape also reminded me of the State Department's claim that the twenty-four T-54/55 tanks in the Nicaraguan arsenal were a threat to Honduras and El Salvador. Lieutenant Colonel John Buchanan (USMC, retired) testified before the House Subcommittee on Inter-American Affairs, the only way to get these tanks to Honduras was to drive them along the Pan-American Highway where they would be an easy target for an air attack.

There is a time-honored tradition among coffee workers that prohibits one from "stealing" berries in another worker's row. The reason for this rule soon became evident to us. Some trees were laden with berries on branches within easy reach. All you had to do was pull the end of the branch down near the center of your basket and with your free hand dislodge the red berries. The taller trees, entangled with the vines and overhanging foliage, were a real struggle. It took twice as long to harvest half as much coffee from these trees. There was a great temptation to slip out of your row to get at one of the smaller trees.

On one occasion I lost contact with the other workers and became a bit apprehensive. I knew that I was not in any danger, but still my mind turned to thoughts of contras and poisonous snakes. The vegetation was so thick around me that I could only see a few feet in any direction. Just as I decided to abandon pride and call out, I heard a bell clanging and a crash in the brush behind me. When I turned around I saw a man pushing his way through the undergrowth and laboriously shifting a box the size of a picnic cooler from a strap across his back to the ground in front of him. He smiled at me, wiped the perspiration from his forehead and asked me if I wanted to buy a popsicle. The scene reminded me of a Woody Allen movie. I bought two.

The next day the vendor didn't bother fighting his way up the slopes to find his customers. All he had to do was to walk along the pathway ringing his bell and the brigadistas came flocking down to meet him. This rugged entrepreneur brought his load of ice cream up from Managua each day for an inexhaustible market.

My daughter became friendly with one family through a ten-year-old girl named Flor de María. She wanted Lisa to help her with her writing skills. Flor was always waiting when Lisa returned from the fields. Her fourteen-year-old brother Dagoberto, one of the guides who took us out to the fields each day, also took a liking to Lisa. The first day he helped her as she struggled with her basket and the tangled vegetation. He worked along with her for the next few days, showing her how to strip the berries and throwing handful after handful into her basket. At the end of the day, he carried her bag down the hill and along the road to the weigh-out station, shuffling along in his worn out heelless shoes. All of this attention stopped abruptly when the older women began teasing him about Lisa.

The family frequently invited Lisa to visit them in their quarters. When they asked what she missed from home, she was embarrassed. "I ended up telling them that I was homesick for sweets," she said, "because everything else seemed so silly when I looked around at what they had." The next day Flor brought her some candy. Lisa continued to receive small gifts of pastries and sweets almost daily from the family.

The night before we left the coffee finca for our three day visit to Managua, we sorted out the possessions that we were going to leave to the local people. The brigade leaders had made it clear that no individual gifts should be given, lest we encourage a demeaning sense of dependency on American handouts. We were soon to discover that no matter how you do it, there is a feeling of awkwardness. The collective donations of medical supplies and tools that went to the clinics or maintenance inventories were no problem, but the personal items such as clothes and shoes posed some difficulties.

Many of us had established friendships with the campesinos and their families. We knew which ones went to work in the thin rubber overshoes and dilapidated footwear. We did not want to leave the decisions about the distribution to an anonymous administrative agency in Managua. The compromise we finally reached was to gather all the clothes and shoes together and then divide them up into individual bundles with the name of a campesino on each. Then we had a ceremony the night before we left and made a group presentation of the bundles.

I still have mixed feelings about that evening. We stood facing the campesiono families who waited politely to hear their names called out. I was pleased that I had been able to direct my work boots to Dagoberto. He recognized them and gave me a smile as he took his bundle. This gave me some satisfaction, but the feeling was soon tempered when we noticed that through some oversight several campesinos received no bundle at all. We looked helplessly across a void infinitely larger than the narrow dirt road between us. After a moment of silence, a spokesperson stepped forward and thanked us for our gifts and our contributions to the harvest. We walked back to the dorm without speaking to each other.

The day we left the farm, I remember feeling pleased with what we had accomplished but relieved that it was over. We went through a delightful reentry into bourgeois comforts when we arrived at the Hotel Ticomo on the outskirts of Managua. Some brigadistas spent the day reveling in the showers and the swimming pool. Some went south to see Masaya. The old marketplace in the Indian barrio there is one of the largest centers of Indian crafts in the country. Others headed to the beach resort at Pochomil.

Located about thirty-five miles from Managua, it rivals any in the world. Kris, my roommate from the farm, said, with a smile, that he was off to study the private sector of the Nicaraguan economy as thoroughly as possible for the next few days.

Lisa and I decided that we would concentrate on Managua. She had heard rumors about a McDonald's somewhere in the city and wanted a fix of junk food as soon as possible. Our first stop was the Intercontinental Hotel, rising up in a pyramid shape above the city. The architecture was a reminder of the prehistoric past when the Mayan and Aztec traders traveled along the shores of Lake Managua. Once inside, we were in the familiar world of the international tourist. Gift shops, car rental desks, coffee shops, and restaurants, all bustling with expensively dressed clientele, completed the shock of our reentry. "Take me to the coffee shop and feed me an expensive, decadent breakfast before I die," Lisa said.

After breakfast we began to explore "downtown" Managua. It was a brief tour, because the 1972 earthquake destroyed most of the central city. This was the second devastating quake in the last fifty years. The city had been destroyed in 1931 and was completely rebuilt. There are three fault lines that intersect under this area. Somoza cited this reason when he announced that the "new Managua" would be built a short distance west of the present city. He prohibited any reconstruction here and began dynamiting the remaining buildings as soon as the National Guard finished looting them. The "new Managua," of course, was never more than a cover for Somoza's theft of the reconstruction aid that poured in. The vacant, rubble-strewn lots, covered with a thin growth of weeds, are a fitting monument to the Somoza dynasty.

As we were walking along, a street cleaner asked us if we were brigadistas. The condition of our clothes gave us away. "How much did you cut?" I was asked.

"About five or six a day," I lied.

"Very good, and you?" he said to Lisa.

"Two, on a good day," she smiled.

"That's O.K." He laughed. "The important thing is that you left your home to come here and help us." His co-workers nodded agreement.

"Five or six a day huh? You owe me a real feast at McDonald's for keeping quiet on that one!" Lisa whispered as we walked away.

By the time we arrived at the small shopping area where this symbol of free enterprise was located, we had covered nearly four miles in the hot sun. The food looked like the stuff in McDonald's here, but the taste, according to Lisa, fell short of her expectations.

We finished our day with a long, leisurely meal at one of the more fashionable restaurants in Managua, where, according to the guide book, "artists, intellectuals, and the international set enjoy conversation and excellent food." Although the conversation was mundane and we saw no celebrities, the food was the kind we had fantasized about as we ate our rice and beans on the farm.

Janet Essley

Dear Nicaragua Exchange:

Here are the evaluations I promised. I participated in the harvest with three different groups of North Americans between November 28 and January 30. The brigades had distinct natures both because of internal structure and the environmental conditions we found ourselves in in Nicaragua. Each one was valuable for different reasons: the first for the cultural exchange with other internacionalistas; the second for the opportunities to learn of the real life of Nicaraguan campesinos; the third, with the Elders Contingent, for the political opportunity to attend the inauguration and to talk with FSLN leadership. The morale of the second group was lowest, and several people of that group expressed disappointment with the brigade.

Gift Giving

This issue surfaced like clockwork on each brigade. It is impossible to ask North Americans not to give gifts to the Nicaraguans with whom we worked. In spite of all verbal orientation, speeches, threats, pleas, reminders, the gifts were still given in all the worst ways. Only by accident and because the group was (a) small, (b) disciplined, (c) mostly involved with internacionalistas, and (d) moved to different UPEs did the first brigade manage to exit Nicaragua without acting like Martian tourist missionaries. Since the gift giving cannot be prevented, it ought to be regulated. The CNSP should be notified to expect this as one of the many problems of North American brigades that has to be weighed in the political decision on extending the invitation.

Another major problem on both the second and third brigades was the consumption of rum, cigarettes, breadstuffs, and the negative effect on the local economy and social structures as a result. All goods should be purchased and shared collectively. Rum and cigarettes especially should be purchased in Managua. This will protect local shopkeepers from overkill and also promote group spirit (and spirits). Foodstuffs brought from the States should be brought with the intention to share not only between North Americans but also with the Nicaraguans, who tend to be forgotten while we worry over our scarcity of spices and sweets.

Following is a list of items we wished we had brought because they could have been so useful to anyone in Nicaragua and would have made our lives at the UPEs better: light bulbs, electrician tape, wire, scissors, jackknives, wrenches, pliers, hammers, nails, sharpening stones, hacksaws, nylon cord, large bowls, two-quart cook pans, tape, glue, whisk brooms, large brooms, children's books in Spanish, large garbage bags, travel towelettes, extra toothbrushes, world maps, maps of Central America, maps of the Western hemisphere, maps of Nicaragua.

As for the Elders Brigade, this group was entirely wonderful. The group functioned well together in an atmosphere of friendship, respect, and joyful solidarity. By comparison to the second brigade composed of college students, the Elders were considerably more patient, flexible, resilient, able to handle adversity, cooperative, politically and culturally sensitive, playful, creative, clean, and hard-working.

Having a large group of Elders presents difficulties for the Nicaraguans, for the younger brigadistas, and for the Elders themselves. There are placement problems (access to medical facilities) and lack of production relative to the amount of personnel required from an UPE to accommodate the group. For the younger brigadistas attached to the Elders contingent, much time can be required in assisting people physically. Some youngers find this frustrating and resent having been placed in this situation. For the Elders themselves, the problems are mostly of self-esteem. Many came with illusions about the difficulty of the work and were disappointed with their capacities to perform. They worked to their limits at the harvest and would not follow orders to "cool it." It was extremely difficult to determine whether or not individuals were working beyond a safe physical stress limit.

The inauguration was wonderful. CNSP arranged buses for us. We made banners that said: "Elders and Youth in solidarity of the United States." As always, everyone seemed to get beyond our poor syntax to the guts of the message. I tried to organize a marching unit and was getting to the point of utter frustration and embarrassment by our lack of discipline, our frivolousness, and our cultural insensitivity, when everyone in the crowd that could see us became very quiet and started clapping for us. Or rather, for the Elders. One more time I was humbled and embarrassed for the quickness of my judgments.

After the inauguration the entire nation was invited to a dance in the stadium down the street. A band was set up, and wild dancing went on into the night. When President Ortega and Fidel Castro went up onto the stage, the crowd went bananas. Yes, all the world loves bananas. And all the people of Nicaragua love Ortega and Castro.

Editor's Note—The Nicaraguan Electoral Process

In Nicaragua, 1984 was an election year, and brigadistas witnessed the electoral process in many forms: sharing the joy of the Sandinista youth brigade in Apascalí at the announcement that the voting age had been lowered to sixteen; attending campaign rallies in several Nicaraguan cities; going with Nicaraguan friends to the polling places; and attending the inauguration ceremonies and national fiesta to celebrate Nicaragua's first democratically elected government in many years.

As with so many stories in this book, the reality that we experienced in Nicaragua is different from the picture presented to us by our government leaders. President Reagan, Secretary of State George Shultz, as well as various contra spokesmen, all said that they wanted to force Nicaragua to hold democratic elections. Those who witnessed the Nicaraguan electoral process know that it was truly democratic. Seven parties participated in the presidential and legislative elections. Due to the structure of Nicaragua's electoral code, all seven parties gained representation in the National Assembly.

One of the first acts of the Sandinistas after the July 19, 1979 triumph was to commit to holding elections no later than 1985. Due to the mounting pressure of the contras and the Reagan/CIA covert war, it was decided to move the date up and to hold the elections two days before the U.S. presidential elections. In order to create the best possible electoral system, the Sandinistas set up three commissions to study electoral procedures in Latin America, Western Europe, and North America. The first two were able to visit and study countries in their assigned regions, but the one assigned to North America was denied visas to visit the United States by the State Department.

When the period of investigation was complete, the Nicaraguans decided to set up a system with proportional representation for the legislative body. It is a system that reflects the actual power of each political party. Nine electoral districts were created throughout the country. Each of the nine districts was given a certain number of candidates to elect, based on population. Region three, the City of Managua, elected twenty-five representatives. Nationally, ninety representatives were elected to the National Assembly.

Every political party had equal access to the media, and an equal amount of money for the campaign was made available to each. Parties were given money according to how many candidates they were putting up for election. Those parties running full slates in all nine districts received 9 million cordobas. Three parties, the Popular Action Movement/Marxist-Leninist, the Nicaraguan Conservative party, and the Nicaraguan Socialist party did not run full slates.

Each presidential candidate of each party was guaranteed a seat in the National Assembly if he received at least 11,000 votes nationally, representing 1 percent of the electorate. All seven parties achieved this minimum. The three other left parties, the Communist, Socialist, and Popular Action parties, have two representatives each in the National Assembly—their presidential candidate and one other.

Women held key positions in the electoral commission and in the whole process of making the elections happen. One of the five members of the Supreme Electoral Council was a woman, as was the Secretary-General of the Council, Rosa Marina Zelaya. Fifty-two percent of all Nicaraguans who voted were women.

Four thousand polling places were set up around the country. Ninety-four percent of those eligible registered and 76 percent of those registered voted. FSLN presidential candidate Daniel Ortega Saavedra received 67 percent of the 1,098,933 votes cast.

Lisa Christensen

February 3

Poverty
>   a word usually referred to as lack of happiness
>   relating to economic wealth
>   therefore associating quantity of money with happiness

Our trip to Managua and Masaya today showed us shocking economic poverty among the poor of Nicaragua. Old wooden shacks, held together by rusty nails and prayer. Floors with no carpets, sometimes not even wood, only dirt.

I think of the United States and wonder why this is so. Today in Masaya we walked for miles in the barrios, visiting and laughing with the peasants and shopkeepers. The spirit of the people—strong, open, and warm—was what made me question what poverty means.

Poverty is an economic condition, not a condition of the soul, of the heart. In my eyes, there is more poverty in the United States than in Nicaragua. The people of Nicaragua make the country what it is today, and while there is economic poverty there is not spiritual poverty—and this is what keeps them going, what their revolution is all about.

Tomorrow I go into the fields to pick coffee for three weeks. While my work is motivated by the economic poverty in Nicaragua, my inspiration comes from the spirit of the people of Nicaragua.

February 6

Today we learned that over the weekend, two West German women brigadistas, doing building reconstruction in Jinotega, were stopped by contras on the road and raped. Several days later, at a press conference, their friends read a statement they wrote saying that now they really feel in solidarity with the people of Nicaragua because they have directly experienced the aggression aimed against them.

Lisa Christensen

Street Poem

tuesday afternoon
eating chicken, potatoes and salad
at an open market

it's a holiday
so many people are out today
the food is a little greasy,
but warm and tasty.
this is our last day here in Nicaragua
as we reflect, collect, and continually search
for clues, stories, answers

halfway through her meal Jeannette is visited
by a thin older woman and her young son
they politely ask if they can finish her meal

for a moment
all thought stops
what to say?
what to feel?

Jeannette suddenly feels full,
and moves down a seat.

Neil Dunaetz

Adoquines are the fitted cobblestones paving many
streets in Nicaragua's cities. Prior to the revolution, Somoza
owned the factory that made them. The insurrectionists
pried them up and stacked them into barricades, behind
which they were able to fight. On a Sunday afternoon trip
to the town of Masaya, I discovered a statue that inspired
the naming of our brigade: a young man wearing a mask

over his face, hurling a rock at the (unseen) National Guard, while standing behind a barricade of adoquines.

We reasoned that we brigadistas were all "products" of the U.S. who had been pried loose by our sense of justice to work in Nicaragua, opposing what our government is trying to do there. One adoquín by itself is not much, but together with many others it helps to build a durable street (or barricade). One brigadista doesn't pick much coffee, but together our contribution is significant. We called ourselves Los Adoquines.

In the cities, the humble and lowly adoquín was an important tool of insurrection. I found that in Nicaragua they celebrate the little things and the common people who form the basis of any real progress. Marco Gonzales, national director of UNAG, said it best when he addressed us our second day in Managua: "This is an ant's war, where we work steady, steady, and do something real big."

Life on the UPE

Our brigade left Managua and traveled south to the hill town of El Crucero. We split into two groups, and my half went to UPE José Benito Escobar. Our new home was a second-story loft, dusty, smoky from the kitchen fires of Nicaraguans who lived in the rooms below us. There was one light bulb that we screwed in and out by hand. We were fortunate to have the company of twenty-eight Baptist students from Managua who had been picking at the UPE for two and a half months.

Visualize sixty-one people sleeping side-by-side on the wood-plank floor, in four neat rows (two on the men's side and two on the women's side), feet dovetailing and not an inch gone to waste!

Coffee is planted on the sides of mountains. It is a vertical world. The "rows" of trees were planted to follow the curve of the mountain. They started and ended in the

Nicaraguan and North American responsables confer upon arrival at UPE José Benito Escobar, February 3, 1985. Photo by Jeff Jones.

most mysterious and confusing places. Some days it was really a jungle.

Coffee berries are very small. You have to pick a lot to accumulate any volume. Often we were given rows that didn't have a lot of berries on the trees, or rows that had very tall trees. This was demoralizing because it meant you had to work harder with less to show for it. But the logic of our two foremen, Francisco and Gustavo, was sound: the best rows were saved for the Nicaraguans whose livelihoods depended on picking large volumes.

There were days when I would forget where I was. I remembered feelings from my youth spent working on farms in Michigan. Most of my fellow brigadistas didn't have this history of losing touch with time and place in the fields to fall back on. However, I noticed one thing that was different: the absence of pressure from above to produce. This was true for the Nicaraguans picking as well as for us North Americans. It was the most relaxed work setting I've ever experienced.

This feeling of freedom in the fields is something new. Prior to the revolution, campesinos were put under tremendous pressures by the owner to produce and to outperform one another. We were told that it was "like slavery, even though it wasn't called that." During a meeting one evening with Gustavo, when asked to tell us what his responsibilities were, he replied that part of his job was to treat people always with respect and not to get upset when they made mistakes, but to remain calm.

On a good day, a Nicaraguan might pick twenty or more medios (a medio is a volume measure, roughly 12 pounds). My best day was twelve medios, but I probably averaged five. Gustavo and Francisco compared us favorably with brigades that had come up from Managua to pick. Personally, I thought we could have picked more than we did. Some people in the brigade weren't very concerned with productivity—after all, the primary reason for the brigade was to work. If it was just a matter of seeing and learning about Nicaragua, there are other programs available.

History of UPE José Benito Escobar

The farm was set up some decades ago by a German owner who called it "Las Delicias." Later it was taken over by Somoza who gave it to one of his National Guard captains. The workers had it very hard then. They were paid according to how strong they were, how much they could produce. The captain offered a two cordoba-a-day bonus to each day's most productive worker. Women were paid half as much as men for the same work. A worker who complained about conditions was fired on the spot. The union did nothing, not even insure that the workers received the legal minimum wage.

There were about 100 people on the farm then. Workers were given four and a half ounces of rice per day. Now they get eleven ounces, and the portion of beans has also been increased. The campesinos had to buy what they needed from a company store. They worked longer hours than they do today.

Insurrectional fighting did not take place on Las Delicias, nor did the people who lived and worked on the farm take an active part in the insurrections of 1978 and 1979. Gustavo related one incident: a National Guardsman came to Las Delicias to arrest an old man who lived and worked there. The old man defended himself and struck the guardsman on the head with his machete. But the guardsman was still able to shoot and kill the old man.

In May of 1979, two months before the victory of the revolution, the captain left the country for Guatemala, abandoning the farm. The workers found themselves without a boss and did not know what to do. So they worked the farm on their own and without pay for the next two months. Shortly after the victory of the revolution, representatives from the ATC arrived and started organizing the workers and the farm.

In 1980, two cousins of the captain showed up, representing his interests. They hired an administrator from Managua to run the farm. They tried to borrow money from the now nationalized national bank and were refused. Citing "lack of money" they suspended work on the farm. Gustavo interpreted this work suspension as an attempt by the cousins to break the new union that was beginning to gather strength.

In 1981, the captain's mother came to Las Delicias and started to run the farm. She brought in new administrators. The agrarian reform department of the revolutionary government began an investigation. The findings were damning to the owner and his relatives. It was discovered that the Bank of America had loaned them money for fertilizers, pesticides, machinery, and repairs, but that this money had been taken out of Nicaragua and not used on the farm. Workers were not being paid for their work, machinery was broken down and not being repaired. The coffee trees were not getting the care they needed, and yields and quality suffered.

Based on the results of its findings, the government decided to take control of Las Delicias in December of 1982, naming the new UPE "José Benito Escobar," after one of the slain FSLN comandantes.

Even with all the confusion and intermittent disruptions of pay, the years from 1981 to 1983 were relatively good ones for the campesinos on the farm. The government first enforced the old minimum wage of twenty-one cordobas per day and then raised the minimum to the current forty-two cordobas per day. Prices remained stable, so there was an overall improvement in purchasing power. As the contra attacks in the north increased during 1983 and 1984, however, prices skyrocketed, and purchasing power shrank accordingly.

A few of the campesinos I talked to said that they are able to buy more today than they could before the revolution. Many more said that in terms of being able to afford what they need, it is just as bad now as it was under the captain and Somoza. Some say that it is worse now—economically—than it was before the revolution.

I saw people without shoes, with clothes so old and worn they were falling off their bodies. A pen or a pencil was a treasure that many didn't have and couldn't afford. Manufactured goods were very dear. What people did have was usually old, worn, and beaten with use. I was especially affected when I saw one older campesino eating his meals out of a used motor oil can. These people weren't living like this out of ignorance, nor out of choice. If they could manage any better, they'd be doing it.

Among the campesinos, I found a general feeling of support for the Sandinistas and the revolution. They understood that it was not the fault of their government that the U.S. is waging a war against them. Even with the material hardships they are experiencing now, they were *all* quick to say that their lives are better now, since the revolution. They can, as they put it, "breathe easier." They have more control over the conditions of their lives.

I didn't see much manifestation of revolutionary fervor on the UPE, except for Lillian and some of the Baptist youth from Managua. The campesinos, both those who live and work there year-round and the migrant workers who leave at the end of the coffee harvest, took their jobs seriously. If you asked them what they thought about things, they would tell you. Clearly they weren't living out most of their dreams. Life was still hard. Some expressed disappointment that many of the benefits that the revolution might have brought are still lacking.

This economic crunch is due to the contra attacks and the U.S. war against Nicaragua. It is the intention of our government to put the country in such an economic squeeze, to make life so miserable for the common people, that they will welcome any change. This is what President Reagan means when he talks about "destabilizing the Sandinista regime." The same thing was done to Chile in the early 1970s. My perspective is that the men who make policy in the U.S., who direct the war machine, have their own agenda. It is based on their own economic interests and objectives, not on the public will. They manipulate public opinion to support their policy objectives rather than letting public opinion determine what they do. The current campaign of misinformation directed against the Sandinistas is a good example. First they decide they want to overthrow the Sandinista government, then they lie to the U.S. people to get us to support their actions.

Eleanor Stein
Thai Stein Jones

Home/work
(Use these words in a sentence.)

A deer is an *animal*.
I have a nice *garden*.
A *stream* runs threw our land.
My father is good at *planting*.

My lover is good at planting.
What is he planting now
in those brown mountains of coffee and war?
He may be planting trees or cotton;
he surely is planting solidaridad
is seeding friendships and memories
that grab the imagination years later.

Surely he is planting and
not picking contra shrapnel.
Not everyone's land has a stream and a garden.
Some people's land has contra and machete-hackers.
You may not know it but your
father is also good at fighting
is also good at simple courage
and doing what has to be done.

Surely it is picking
beans or bolls
and bringing back semillas of mobilizing and uprising.

Surely it is coming home.

Harvest Brigades, 1984–1985   /   169

Sister Sheila Murphy

I try to read other than the *New York Times*. I read the *National Catholic Reporter*. I try to read *America*, sometimes *Sojourners*, so that I get a broader perspective than just what Washington wants us to read or hear or believe.

I had gone to Riverside Church to see the movie "El Norte." I picked up a brochure for the brigades, but I saw that they were during school time. Either I didn't put it down when I thought I had, or someone gave me another, but when I got home, I found that I still had it. I spoke to my pastor and he was very supportive. I talked to my eighth grade teacher, who becomes acting principal in my absence. When I'm away, she takes over. When she found out that for seventy dollars more I could stay for a whole month, she said, "Don't worry. Go and have a good time, and then come back and settle down."

On the plane coming down from New York, two women sitting next to me asked me how long I was going to stay in Miami. Rob and Paul were in front of me, and they seemed to turn around when they heard the question. I said, "I'm not going to Miami, I'm going to Nicaragua." The five of us got into a lengthy discussion about what was going on. They weren't totally unaware and they really were interested. They gave us their addresses; they wanted to hear from us. They wished us well and said they would pray for us. It was really exciting to know that what we were doing was arousing interest and concern even before we got there to do it. It gives you hope that if our people knew a little more of the other side, they might act in a different way.

On Sunday, I went into Managua to deliver a box of medicines to a friend of a friend from the Bronx. I called them from a phone at the Hotel Intercontinental. They picked us up and entertained us for the afternoon. They were super gracious, most hospitable: it was wonderful to get first-hand information. The father especially was very supportive of the revolution, very positive. Their neighbor, on the other hand, was not so supportive. She was also visiting at the house. She came over and sat by me and said, "Now sister, I don't want to offend you, but I do not support the revolution." She was not a Sandinista. The reason, I thought, given my limited ability to communicate in Spanish, was the conscription of the youth. The sending them out to fight. Which I can understand. Any parent would be concerned about having their son go to war.

The father feels that they have something of value in Nicaragua and that they have to fight for it. He said if they send for him, if they extend the age limit up to include him, he would go.

Wendy Wallas

Tell us about your experiences as a brigade leader.

Well, that's easy. It was an exceptional group. Even though I've never been a leader of a group like that before, I found people to be responsible, responsive to suggestions that I made. I loved feeling that it was my job to watch out for people and take care of them. I loved it when people would come up to me and say, "So-and-so's having a hard time," or tell me what their problems were.

Did anyone ask you how you were doing?

Brigadista Wendy Wallas harvesting coffee at El Crucero. Photo by Jeff Jones.

People did that a lot. Because my Spanish is weak, I depended on several others to translate and help me communicate, and that helped to prevent it from becoming too hierarchical or autocratic a situation. Heidi and Nancy did all the translating in the fields. And Michael really outdid himself by being not only health responsable, but by being my coleader. He gave me a lot of support. He never impinged on my role. So I didn't feel separate from the group.

Did you hear about Maude, how she got to the flat coffee picking land? She has had a lot of medical problems. In fact, she told me that she had not told us about them beforehand because she knew that we would not have wanted her to come on the brigade. One of the days that we went very far up into the hills she just couldn't handle it.

The next morning when I woke up I saw she was already up and talking to Michael. She told him that she would go out and try to make it one more time but that, if she couldn't, she would go back to Managua and leave. That day was another long hike, three to four miles down a canyon and then up into the hills. And she couldn't make it. She had to turn back. All day I was feeling so sad, thinking that she would be leaving.

When we got back, Lisa, who had been sick and stayed behind, said: "Maude got it all worked out. One of the campesinos gave her a flat place to pick." A little later Maude came up from the fields and told me what happened. Maude doesn't speak a word of Spanish, but she said, "I just went out there and showed them that I had some problems and couldn't pick with the rest of the brigade." And they were great and understood and gave her a flat area to pick in. They set her up in this spot, and she would grab her lunch as the cart went by. She did it every day. When people were recovering from being sick, they would go and pick with Maude for a day. She was an incredible asset for the group. It was her idea for us to give Candida, the cook, a day off by having us prepare the food for the whole UPE one day.

Did you ever speak to the group about laxness, productivity, attitudes?

Toward the end of the first week I was worried about a lax attitude developing. Some people were finding the work very difficult. I didn't give a very intense talk. Someone had made contact with the other group, and the word came back that they were really into production over there. Of course they had better picking than we did in the beginning. Michael, who had lost his voice, wanted me to say some words about everyone being productive. But my heart wasn't really in it. I felt that, if everyone went out and worked all day, there wouldn't be a need to push for increased productivity. I also felt that, if people got sick or just needed a break, that was fine. I didn't want it to be a situation where people felt free to just stay in camp and hang out, but I also didn't want this heavy thing where you've got to work, work, work. It never really got to be a problem.

Was there ever any debate about whether each day's cut should be tallied up collectively or individually?

It ended up pretty loose. Some of us picked together and combined bags during the day so we wouldn't have to carry as much all over the hillsides. Ed was probably the best picker in our group. He was older than most of us and had a son on one of the navy ships stationed off the Nicaraguan coast. He hustled everyday and filled his sack and kept his tally true for himself. One day Dave picked thirteen measures, and the campesinos called him "El Tigre."

I remember, sometime during the second week, realizing that I had been so absorbed in the brigade that I had not thought about home at all. It was shocking to me that my normal life had not come into my consciousness for so long.

The day we made the dinner was great. For several hours in the dining room, we were all sitting around together, more than at any other time. We were sitting there chopping vegetables. Tom Fryer, who had been a cook in the navy, was working with the giant pots they had, trying to figure out proportions to cook for over 100 people on the open fire. We didn't want to buy out the little merchants in El Crucero, so we went to the Empresa and asked them to get the food for us from Managua, which they did.

Michael made a rice pudding. We put in bananas and then people started bringing out all the little goodies that they had stored in their packs, like dried fruit and raisins. The little campesino children stood around the pot while the pudding was cooling, practicing saying "rice pudding" in English. We were all laughing. It was a fabulous afternoon.

Brenda Grove

February 21, 1985

Hola:

Estoy enferma. For the past two days my temperature has been between 103 and 105 (with aspirin). Finally it went back to normal last night. But yesterday the diarrhea started and that continues. At least today I have the strength to get up and crawl down the stairs to the outhouse. By last night, my spirits were so low I just wanted to be home. I couldn't have handled another day with the fever.

By the time the student brigade left on Friday, a number of friendships had been formed. We had a party Thursday night, bringing our tapes and polaroid camera downstairs. Friday night, when the bus came for them, there was a long round of hugs and address exchanges and, after they boarded, holding hands through the windows. As the bus began to roll, about ten of us sat in front of it chanting "NO PASARAN!" The bus stopped and there was a moment of silence. We weren't sure if the driver saw the humor in this. Suddenly all the students piled out of the bus for one more round of goodbyes. It sure felt empty around here that night with only the thirty of us.

The students have been coming back out from Managua to visit, and, last Saturday night, Lisa and I went to Managua with Zoroyada and Bismark (brother and sister) and stayed at their house overnight. It's a three room house for three kids, parents, and grandfather. They have a TV, refrigerator, running water from a hose, and a large bookcase full of books. Their father is a lawyer and in the military, stationed in Matagalpa. He comes home on Sundays. Both parents are very pro-Sandinista. Sunday we went to a church service where Gianni (the students' leader and the guitar player at the UPE) was the minister.

We took a group polaroid picture and put it on a big poster that we're going to give to the campesinos the night we cook them dinner. The poster, translated, will say: We of the International Brigade Los Adoquines offer this dinner as a concrete expression of our solidarity with our friends at the UPE José Benito Escobar. Our experiences on this farm have taught us much about the life of Nicaraguan campesinos. We will always remember our friends here who have shown us so much affection, respect, and patience. When we return to the United States, we will continue to work together with you for peace in your country and for the future of your children. Although a large distance will separate us, we will always be together in spirit.

February 25, 1985

The dinner was a great success. Two light bulbs were found for the occasion so we could see the food and each other for a change. Our poster was on the wall. One of the Nicas read it to the group and then asked us for some of the same paper. A few of them went off and came back with a message for us. It said: From the workers and campesinos of this UPE, José Benito Escobar, we want to tell you that it fills us with happiness to know that there has been so much understanding and affection between the brigadistas and ourselves. At the same time, it fills us with sadness to know that our international friends are leaving to go back to their country. But we know that we will always remember you with affection and friendship because you have taught us about the lives of campesinos in your country. We hope that soon we will be able to live together again.

Reverend Otis Lee

My name is Otis Lee. I am the minister at Christ's Lutheran Church in St. Paul, Minnesota. I have five children, and to me it's a big sadness that none of them have come down to Nicaragua. They grew up in Brazil, where we lived for ten years, so Latin America is old hat to them. They are concerned about making their own livings.

We have an old-time congregation in downtown St. Paul. We used to be larger, but many people have moved away to the suburbs. Now we have many Cambodian and Hmuong refugees, and some Ethiopians. It's a very mixed racial group and very exciting for that reason. The refugees are not Lutherans. We have just provided a sanctuary where they can come. We don't try to force anything upon them, but they seem to like our love and concern, so they stick around.

Most of the congregation are uninformed about U.S. policy in Central America. The remaining whites of Norwegian and Swedish descent are mostly elderly, and they just don't seem to have any interest at all. The refugees are caught in between. Here the U.S. has offered them asylum and help. Last Sunday, though, when I told the congregation of my plan to come here, some of the most positive support I got I could read in the eyes of the Cambodians. They know something of what it means to suffer under regimes like those in Guatemala, El Salvador, and the old Somoza dictatorship.

I came here to show my solidarity with the people of Nicaragua. One of the things that has impressed me most is what they're doing for the poor and oppressed. To me, that's what Christianity is all about.

Reverend Kathryn Lee

The Admirable Experiment of Nicaragua's Sandinistas

I am one of the many who have journeyed to Nicaragua. Daily I read newsletters, articles, and news stories from the area. The stories in the national news media often present a different picture than I see in other correspondence. What can I believe?

From the conflicting voices in Nicaragua, I choose to give my support to those who live there and have known it for many years. Ignacio Hernandez is director of the Bible Society of Nicaragua. He said, "The government leaders haven't asked us any questions about our distribution of almost 500,000 New Testaments. There is no problem with the government; 20,000 copies of the Fourth Gospel were distributed to the army."

Fernando Cardenal, director of the literacy crusade, has been denied his priestly function because of his government post. He said, "It would be a terrible blow for the church if one or another of us (priests) abandoned the revolution, for then the church would not be present to bear witness to God. I feel deeply the call of God in the suffering and cries of our people in poverty, and for this revolution I'm ready to shed the last drop of my blood."

Last November a group of Brazilian Lutheran pastors from the Río de Janeiro area wrote an open letter to President Reagan saying, in part, "We urge you to suspend

"The Admirable Experiment of Nicaragua's Sandinistas" by the Reverend Kathryn Lee. *Minneapolis Star and Tribune,* April 13, 1985. Reprinted with permission.

immediately the threats of intervention, of the pressure direct and indirect exercised by the United States against the government elected by the people of Nicaragua."

With an editorial writer in the *Boston Globe*, I believe, "The Sandinistas are engaged in a serious, popular, mostly well-intentioned and frequently competent national experiment not altogether unlike our own revolution, though set in a very different, and far more difficult context. For America to try to destroy such a revolution out of fear that its example will awaken the downtrodden in other nations is a contemptible historical wrong."

Steve Emerman

Does Nicaragua have the potential to develop its own energy resources?

Yes. Nicaragua is cooking. Any country that has so many volcanoes, such high heat flow, and hot springs, has tremendous geothermal potential. There is a plant on Momotombo that has been successful. It has a thirty-five megawatt capability, which is substantial.

Who built the plant? Did they have foreign help?

They had some Italian help. Actually the program started under Somoza. Some research was done. Somoza passed a law that if someone drilled into your land and nothing came of it, you were reimbursed an incredible amount of money. So he just drilled all over his own land.

He was just drilling empty holes and then writing himself checks from the treasury. That was the extent of his geothermal program. Then the Sandinistas took it over and turned it into a working plan.

Is there other energy potential?

Yes. Oil and gas, both on shore and off shore. I've heard this from a number of different sources. To develop an oil field from scratch you're talking about a lot of money, at least a billion dollars.

You said that they had a goal of transforming all their energy to geothermal by 1990.

I said the goal was to shut down the oil burning plants by 1990. There is also hydropower and biomass. For example, along with sugar cane, you grow eucalyptus trees. They grow very fast. When the sugar mills aren't operating, you burn the eucalyptus for power.

Will they reach the goal by 1990?

It wouldn't surprise me if they've given up on that goal because of the war.

Annie Borgenicht

Our first two days in Nicaragua were spent at a hotel in the hills south of Managua. We were having orientation sessions and getting to know one another. The second night, just as I was falling asleep, another brigadista woke me with the news that there was a woman in labor in the hotel's front office. She lives three or four kilometers up the road from the hotel. She was having her third child. Her first two children were delivered by a midwife at home seven and nine years ago. The midwife had recently died. She was registered with a hospital in Managua.

She went into labor early that morning, then thought it wasn't the real thing. Later, she had no transportation, so she started walking. She got as far as the hotel. We got together the medical equipment and supplies we had brought and prepared to do the delivery. The people at the hotel called an ambulance, which arrived very quickly, maybe in ten or fifteen minutes. She got to the hospital in Managua in time.

This trip to Nicaragua was a long time in coming. I had many years of political work behind me. Several of my closest friends had traveled there on tours, to attend language school, or on their own. My first choice was to work as a nurse. However, this required more time than I could allow. So my desire to do concrete work led me to the harvest brigades.

We were sent to work on a state farm close by Managua. The second night at the UPE, as I walked up the hill, I was stopped by a young campesino couple. They wanted to talk about life in the U.S. They wanted to know what it was like to live in peace. They were hooked by the dream and illusion that material wealth gives of the good life. I explained the constant tension and fear that resides in us. The constant vigilance that we must keep in our homes, in the streets, against robbery, rape, murder. I tried to explain our war at home. I told them that when you live in a society so filled with material goods, selfishness thrives.

We talked about the world generally being in economic disorder. I shared stories about the growing number of homeless on the streets in the U.S. They did not feel directly touched by the revolutionary process. When asked about the government, they said they felt separate and that politics did not have much to do with their lives.

I was struck by the lack of political education and change on the farm where we lived. I had spoken with brigadista friends from last year who worked side by side with Sandinista youth. Their spirit and support of the revolutionary process had been a strong influence. We had little exposure to this. When I met a revolutionary Nicaraguan who worked with us for awhile, I asked him about this. Concerned, he reminded me that this was a country at war on many fronts. The major battles were in the north and the south. The whole country was mobilized to support the front. Cultural workers, students, factory workers, all who could be, were working at the front. Everyone was working in the harvests or battling the contras.

Most of our energy as brigadistas went into coffee production, and survival. On very basic levels, our physical survival was tested. We were staying in a large barn-like structure over 100 years old. It is very difficult to describe this house. We lived there with about seventy-five campesinos. Some were there for the coffee harvest, and some families lived there year round. The building had one long corridor. On each side were covachas. This word translates as small cave, hut, shanty, cubbyhole, or small dark room. They were the size of piano crates. There were about forty-five of them, two levels high. They housed families. There were a few empty covachas that some of the brigadistas stayed in. Most gravitated to the top of the upper level, right below the slanted roof. There was constant noise and one light bulb in the building that was kept on all night. I, who had wanted to be in Nicaragua for such a long time, woke up the first morning, after hours of broken sleep, turned to a friend and said: "If this doesn't get any better, I'm not going to make it." Fortunately she had been on a brigade before and was able to ignore my comment. She knew we would adjust and learn.

Coffee beans drying on the patio at UPE José Benito Escobar. Photo by Jeff Jones.

After awhile a group of us began to sleep on the large concrete patio where the coffee beans were raked out for drying. There was a guard there all night who walked among us with his old rifle to guard the coffee and mill. I know we added spice to his nightly walks. I can only imagine how quiet the UPE must be now. The harvest has ended, the campesinos and brigadistas have left. Only the year-round families remain, picking up the last of the spilled beans from the hillsides, pruning the trees, and maintaining the mill.

Another of our coping mechanisms for life on the UPE presented problems. There was one restaurant within walking distance of the farm. Several of us went up there the first Sunday after a week of coffee picking. The owner wanted payment in dollars. We tried as a group to make it a policy not to patronize the restaurant. However, by the time we understood enough of the economic problems of using dollars, many had integrated the meals there as a way of surviving the limited diet on the UPE. The "black market" is eating away internally at the Nicaraguan economy. It plays the role of middle-man, inflating prices and increasing the shortages of basic goods.

Returning to the States is painful. All the news reports of President Reagan's determination to continue his war against the people of Nicaragua have spurred my determination to get out and talk to people about what I have seen. Despite the separate worlds that we live in, there are powerful bridges being built between us. I carry within me now a lot of the strength of the Nicaraguan people who continue to fight long and hard for what they know is theirs to have: their land and lives in freedom.

Antonio Flores

What changes have occurred at your farm since the triumph of the revolution?

The main change since 1979 is health care. Before, there was none provided in the haciendas. When a worker was sick, they received half pay. Today, access to health care has improved. Year round workers receive a full day's pay for a certain number of sick days.

The rights of workers are respected more. You can't be fired without a good reason. Before, you could be jailed for complaining about the patrón (the owner of the farm). There were some patrones who tried to be good to the workers before the revolution. They would be pressured by the other owners. Some were even killed for this reason.

We are especially happy to have foreign brigades here. It gives us a chance to get to know other people as people. Before, the only Nicaraguans who met foreigners were the owners, the rich. The people were as nothing. Now we can talk to all kinds of people, person to person, so that people of other countries might know that we're a good people who want to work hard and live a better life. Now every campesino has the opportunity to visit other countries. Our government has programs for this purpose. Also, many campesinos have had the opportunity to be trained as technicians, even to go to higher education, to be doctors. This is very important to us, why many of us support our government so strongly.

James W. Lahey

Anecdotes by a Coffee Cutter in Nicaragua

Years of observing U.S. involvement in Nicaragua nurtured a shame in me. I felt responsible for the deaths of innocent families, simply by paying my taxes. I was going to see whether my interpretations of the problems there were based in fact, or were a reflexive or emotional fabrication of my mind.

Strangers in this land, we offloaded. The peasants watched from a distance as we piled our trappings in front of a large stone shed. I felt clumsy during those moments and sensed my appearance was belligerent. In my self-consciousness, I became preoccupied with where to place my pack and how to place my feet among the litter. The everpresent green smoke chased us in the fierce wind that was suddenly there, and before our eyes the yellow dust applied its first of many layers—and we began to blend in.

There is a caterpillar in the coffee fields of Nicaragua called la polla. It feeds on coffee leaves and is rather large. It resembles a Pekingese dog in miniature, and its red hairs deliver enough neurotoxin to cause extreme pain and temporary paralysis of the arm and chest. Francisco, our macheteman, says when you get stung to quickly find two leaves from different trees, rub them together, place them behind one ear, then forget about the whole thing.

The lunch wagon arrives in the coffee fields at UPE José Benito Escobar. Photo by Jeff Jones.

A tarantula crawled into my sleeping bag last night. I was reading and it stepped up onto my book. In horror, I flicked it hard, but instead of propelling it into the darkness, I managed to have it come back onto me and into the sleeping bag. I went crazy in silence and killed it with the book I was reading.

We think we had mule tonight. Greg says he saw the head out back. Greg has been here two months. He met the group of elders that were here in January and he said he was humbled by the experience. "I expected them to have heart attacks!" he exclaimed wildly. "But one, named Sarah, seventy-six years old, hobbled two miles up the mountain every morning. And with a sprained ankle, for chrisakes!"

I worked alone this morning. High on a hogsback I watched the morning fog fill the canyon to overflowing and wash up over me like soft ocean breakers. The shouts of "Oia! Oia!"—usually sharp signals between the campesinos—seemed far away and muted. Though I knew some of them were just below me.

The picking was better there than it had been in days. As I worked in the chill dampness, I thought of Joan and of my family and of how committed I felt during those hours alone. I thought, too, of the children I have met here and the likelihood that they will die in the war or of some disease.

The morning passed and the sun arched high and, together with the incessant wind, tore holes in the fog and the day warmed, then turned hot.

Francisco and Gustavo are our machetemen. To show where he wants you to work, Francisco will pivot his sinewy frame and carve his machete through the air in one smooth and deliberate motion. Gustavo, on the other hand, is shy and timidly waves his machete off in the direction of the forest.

One late afternoon, I thought I was alone while lugging a ninety pound sack of coffee berries up from the bottom of a steep ravine. Believing I was far from any pathway, I was startled by the sudden and quiet appearance of Francisco. My head was bent downward by the load, but I could see him move the machete from his right to his left hand. As I passed, he patted me softly on the shoulder and said, "Bueno," then sliced the air in slow motion in the direction of the nearest pathway to the top.

Francisco just returned from market. I went down to get water, and he was seated with his three children surrounding him. He was counting into each little hand two small pieces of colored candy. He looked up at me as I passed, but he didn't smile.

The fog was thick as soup at dawn. Threading our way along a narrow trail into a canyon, three men with some dogs burst silently from the edge dragging a coati they had just killed. One of the men peered through the pale at me for approval, and I nodded and said, "Sí. Muy bueno." A dog

Lunch is served at UPE José Benito Escobar. Photo by Jeff Jones.

looked up at the man then down at the limp coati. I watched it happen in front of me but none of it was of this place or time, as if I were looking through a dusty glass case in a forgotten corner of an old museum. As I walked away, I turned and looked over my shoulder. But just as I expected, there was nothing there.

At home in the United States, we read about U.S. citizens who fly to Honduras to fight as mercenaries alongside the contras. But the ones we don't learn about are those who fly to Nicaragua to fill in as computer programmers, as surgeons, school teachers, scientists, nurses, auto mechanics, builders, foresters, economic advisers, lawmakers, agrarians, harvesters. These "civil mercenaries" come from around the world as evidence that more and more of the world's population is awakening to the historical importance of Nicaragua's thrust into the present as a new republic.

The "Big Pine III" maneuvers have begun, and when they are over, one and a half years of new military equipment will be left in the hands of the contras. Nicaragua has once again gone on alert. At night in front of the bombed out cathedral in Plaza de la Revolución, I witness 85,000 militia—men, women, and children—sing the Sandinista hymn. And I sense by the strength in their voices and the unbidden tears in their eyes that they will fight to the last individual before giving up their hard-earned right to remain free.

Paul Griffin

When I was a teenager, I was idealistic and socially concerned. I became aware of U.S. policy in Vietnam and joined the antiwar movement. This exposed me to a community of people with a beautiful vision of what society and human relationships might be. I was certain that, if only the hawks in the government and the hardhats among the population could feel the spirit of love and cooperation I felt among the antiwar people, they'd be won over, the war would end, and society would in some way be reborn.

Of course, the story unfolded differently. My government would not be so easily moved. The events of my personal life seemed to parallel and reflect the larger turmoil, frustration, and despair that many people went through.

The triumph of the revolution in Nicaragua in 1979 perked my interest, and I tried to follow events through various news media, harboring a quiet hope that here something real and something good might be happening. With President Reagan's escalating aggression going from bad to worse, I found myself sickening at the thought that whatever gains had been made thus far against such obstacles would be reversed. When I learned of the opportunity to do volunteer work on a harvest brigade, I jumped at the chance.

Before I came, I studied the history of Nicaragua, the story of the popular insurrection that succeeded in overthrowing Somoza. I tried to find out the intentions of the Sandinistas as leaders of this revolution. As impressed as I was with what I learned by reading, I'm overwhelmed at the generosity and determination of the people I have met here. These are people mobilized on their own behalf, committed in an effort to attain self-sufficiency and self-determination.

They have been gracious enough to allow me to participate in their historic moment, and this has given my own life a sense of significance and purpose.

The government here encourages idealism in its young people, and provides them practical channels for its direction. I am grateful to the Nicaraguan people for these lessons, for their inspiration. I feel that I am, once again, part of something larger than myself.

North American and Nicaraguan student brigadistas take a break from coffee picking at UPE José Benito Escobar. Photo by Jeff Jones.

Judith Holton Rew

Dear Family and Friends:

I have just returned from my third trip to Nicaragua. This time I went as leader of a volunteer cotton brigade similar to the group I was a member of last January. I went to Nicaragua to demonstrate support for the country and to help make up for its very critical shortage of farm labor. I returned with admiration and love for the growing number of Nicaraguans I count as friends; respect for the country's leaders who stubbornly continue to forge a humane and democratic future for their people in the face of incredible economic and military obstacles; and, finally, rage and sadness that these obstacles were put into place by the U.S. government and maintained by my tax dollars.

For the past five years, the Nicaraguan people have worked to build a system of health care, education, land, and food for everybody, within a society where the arts, community, and religion flourish. But this "process," as the Nicaraguans call it, is at a standstill because of the war being waged on the country's borders.

The casualties of this war are people like my friend Luis, nineteen years old, and his working-class family in Managua. I met him last year when he was spending his summer running a mobile library throughout the countryside. Since his teens, he has volunteered for every project imaginable. He is now in the army, and the last his family heard from him he was mobilized in the mountains on a dangerous military mission against the contras. When I saw his mother at church last Sunday, she thanked me for being a friend to Luis and gave me a jar of homemade jelly. She told me how proud she is of him. She had the look, however, of any mother who knows her son might not return alive.

The methods the contras use don't surprise Nicaraguans. They are the same methods used for fifty years by Somoza's forces. This was attested to by Francesca, a sixty-year-old woman I visited in the northern city of Estelí. She has been active in the struggle since the 30s. Before the victory in 1979, Francesca ran a "safe house" where Sandinistas could hide. The house was discovered by the National Guard one night. They attacked and murdered a famous Sandinista leader, José Benito Escobar, and beheaded her own son before her eyes. Her pregnant daughter fled and later gave birth to a son, all alone.

While in Estelí, we visited a beautiful, well-equipped orphanage and heard story after story of tragedy. When we told Francesca about our visit, she said, "There are so many orphans now, they can't even be counted."

Life is very hard in Nicaragua. I was shocked at the difference between now and a year ago. Prices have doubled. The poor have fewer clothes to wear. Since schools and medical centers are routinely destroyed by the contras, most construction in the countryside has stopped. Nine new schools, built by volunteers, dot the countryside around León where I was picking cotton. All nine stand roofless because of the shortage of materials.

One very poor family invited some friends, a group of British construction workers, and me to a lunch of stewed chicken and yucca. The mother pulled me aside and said, "Life is beautiful in Nicaragua, so beautiful. If it weren't for the poverty I would have no complaints. But the poverty.... The poor have one choice: they can eat or have clothes. Never both."

How many times have I heard that phrase, "Life would be beautiful if it weren't for..." A year ago I was struck by the fierce and jubilant pride of a people who believed in their right to self-determination. This year I find the joy and pride infused with anger and sadness. The contras' chief aim—and the U.S. government's—is to demoralize the people through poverty and violence.

Nicaragua has filled its labor gap with what is called "rojinegro" (black and red—the colors of the Sandinista flag), voluntary work performed by students, professionals, churches, and neighborhood organizations from the cities, who go to the countryside for a Sunday afternoon, week, or several months to cut the coffee and cotton. This system has served to maintain production and also to break down historic barriers between country and city dwellers.

My brigade had to travel by cotton trailer, or by foot, the three miles to and from the field where we worked. We got a true taste of the long, grueling day of a farm worker. Living and working so far apart, we got to know the countryside and made many friends along the way.

Among our new friends were a group of prisoners at one of Nicaragua's open prisons. It was basically a bunkhouse like ours, with no walls, no gates, no guards except for one chaperone. The prisoners walked to and from the fields, just like us, swinging their machetes. The only reason we noticed them at all was that they were dressed in blue outfits in much better condition than most clothing we saw around us. We talked to them about their lives. They were mostly ex-National Guardsmen who had received five year sentences and would soon be released. The Sandinistas had treated them more than kindly, recognizing the difference between a real Somocista and an uneducated peasant cajoled into fighting on the wrong side. In prison, they received education and job training. They were very kind to us and enjoyed the attention.

This was not the first time that I was impressed by the compassion shown by the Sandinistas toward their enemies. I met a U.S. priest in Managua whose main interest is prisons. He confirmed that this one was no exception. Nicaragua needs people to live and work productively; therefore, the Nicaraguan penal system is based on rehabilitation.

Since returning to the States, several people have asked me if there is religious freedom in Nicaragua. I can only state it plainly: freedom of religion is a legal right guaranteed in the FSLN's Document on Religion, issued shortly after the Triumph of July 19, 1979. Churches operate freely and are of many faiths. I know of Catholic, Moravian, Evangelical, Mormon, and Presbyterian. Three priests, Ernesto Cardenal, Fernando Cardenal, and Miguel D'Escoto, hold major government positions. Christian "base communities" were a major force in the Revolution and continue to be among its most devoted workers.

The kind of Christianity that flourishes in Nicaragua is special. It is an open, participatory kind of Christianity that incorporates a lot of singing and clapping and patriotism. The "peasant mass" that is practiced at the church I attend when I am there, Santa María de Los Angeles, begins with a song that, for me, sums up the question of religion in Nicaragua:

You are the God of the poor,
the human and simple God.
The God who sweats in the street,
The God with dark and weathered skin.
This is why I talk to you
the way I talk to my own people.
Because you are God the laborer,
Christ the worker.

My brigade worked at El Carmen, a farm made up of nine families. One evening we held a get-acquainted meeting. We all sat in a big circle and introduced ourselves. They had many questions about us, and we wanted to learn more about them. Some had fought in the Revolution; others had come to El Carmen precisely to escape the fighting in León. Most of them now worked as cotton pickers. We asked one young boy in his early teens to tell us what he wanted to be when he grew up. He was very timid, so his mother stood up and said, "Tell them. Tell them how you hate to pick cotton. Tell them how you want to study in León to become an engineer. The Revolution gives you that right, you know!" A teenage girl explained that she wanted to go to business school to learn to be a secretary. These are remarkable goals for the children of peasants.

Finally we asked a younger child to tell us what she thought of the Revolution. She flung her arms open and said, "Some of it I like, and some of it I don't. We go to school now and we didn't before the Revolution and that's good. But some of it is just talk, talk, talk!" We all laughed, including the parents.

Maxine Shaw

I was one of the translators on the Fannie Lou Hamer Brigade. We made many wonderful friends in Nicaragua, but one stands out. He was a recruiter for the militia who lived near the farm where we stayed. We had a lot of political conversations with him.

We found him interesting to talk to because he had a lot of information. In one conversation, someone asked him a question about religion. He mentioned how the Catholic church had been very progressive, how many people had come to the Revolution through the theology of liberation, including himself. But many of the protestant sects, he said, had been basically counterrevolutionary. We laughed, and someone told him about Jerry Falwell. We told him who Falwell was and some of the things he was against. We mentioned Falwell's attitude toward gay people, since many of us were gay. He laughed and said, "Well, of course, that's no longer a problem in our country." He said that in his view, homosexuality was a symptom of oppression and that, since there no longer was oppression in Nicaragua, they no longer had the *problem* of homosexuality. We stared at him in disbelief. Everything he had said up until then made perfect sense, but we weren't going to let him feed us that line.

We challenged him on it right then. We didn't get very far at first. He maintained his view that it was a sickness, a symptom of a sick society. Finally one of the nongay brigadistas asked him, "Are you aware that gays and lesbians are in the forefront of the solidarity movement in our country?" And he said "No." Then we asked him if he was aware that many of us were gay (we had named ourselves the Harvey Milk squad of the Fannie Lou Hamer brigade). And he said no. He stopped for a moment, with a blank look. Then he said, "Well, if you are in solidarity with us, then I guess you are welcome."

We kept on talking for a while. By the end of the conversation, his view had gone from defining gayness as a problem to defining it as an *issue*. We thought that was progress. But it didn't stop there. The next day, Gerry gave him a copy of the *Gay Community News* from Boston with an article by some members of a previous brigade. He sat there reading it while we were eating breakfast. That was when we learned that he could speak and read English. The next day he asked to borrow a dictionary. He said "I'm really trying to read this newspaper, and I'm having trouble with a lot of the words." I laughed and said, "The words you're having trouble with are probably not in the dictionary." I said I'd tell him the words, but he said no, that he really wanted to study it. So I loaned him my dictionary.

The next day he came over to where we were living and asked us if we had a couple of hours to talk. We said sure. He sat down with us and said, "I really want to understand. I want to understand it as a political movement and I want to understand it on a personal basis." He said, "You're challenging my stereotypes." He said that he had always had a view of homosexuals as decadent and the dregs of society. He could not see how such people could contribute to society in any way. Then he told us that we did not seem that way to him, since we had done a lot of talking and he had seen us working hard in the cotton fields. He said, "I respect you."

We talked for a long time, and he asked many questions. Some were very naive, like "What is the relation of your movement to the nudist movement?" And we said, "The what?" A lot of his questions reflected the basic antigay stereotypes. For example, "If you are gay, does that mean you will sleep with anyone?" One woman with us told him that she and her lover had been together for fifteen years. That blew his mind. He was also amazed to learn that I had two sons.

Gerry talked to him about how we were a political movement of oppressed people, that a lot of gay people were in the solidarity movement because they had experienced oppression, and could identify with the Nicaraguans.

Finally he said to us that, on a personal level, he had changed his views and that, on a political level, he wanted to study the question more. We were talking about how there really are a lot of gay people, and he admitted that given Nicaraguan culture and Latin culture there probably were a lot of gay Nicaraguans "in the closet." Women had made important gains through the Revolution because of their open participation in it. But he told us that he had never heard of a homosexual participating openly in the Nicaraguan liberation struggle. Then someone made a joke saying, "Hey, you might even have a gay person in your family." He suddenly got very quiet. Then he said, "Well, I did have someone in my family who was bisexual. But he was killed by the Somocistas when I was a teenager. It was my brother." We were amazed and asked him why he had his views when it was his own brother. And he said, "Until now, that's the only way I knew of to understand him."

Kathleen Donahoe

How do you evaluate your experience in Nicaragua?

I don't know yet all that it means. I am just beginning to see some of the possibilities. I had a dream last week—there were no images, only words and feelings—something like "I cannot support the U.S. in any way. I oppose all that it stands for. I have no right to continue as a U.S. citizen, enjoying those privileges and, just by being here, supporting all that I now find morally reprehensible." When I woke up, I felt very strongly that I must move to Nicaragua. That, I hope, is my most extreme reaction.

The others decrease in degree of lifestyle change, all the way down to picking up where I left off and continuing on the same level of involvement as before. Ask me again next year, or better yet three or four years down the line, and perhaps I will be able to give you a definite answer on what it has meant. Right now, all I can say is, it has made real for me some things, like imperialism, which I had previously heard only as a rhetorical word; and it has me in a moral dilemma—somewhat confused, somewhat frustrated, somewhat hopeful, and somewhat scared—about what to do, how to live my life consistent with what I have learned.

Michael Rozyne

The brigade experience gave me colors, smells, tastes, faces, dust, and sweat to fill into my previous skeletal image of Nicaragua. It gave me a look inside myself that I never seem to take when immersed in my everyday skin. I filled fifty journal pages effortlessly. The brigade was, to my great surprise, very relaxing. For two weeks, I rose with the

Ric Mohr

roosters to an already determined day—cotton, cotton, and then a siesta. No decision to make about the day's plans. Hard work. Heat. Waiting. And lots of time for reflection.

The brigade settled twenty-five people in the small pueblo of El Carmen. And for two weeks we were able to pretend that we were neighbors, sharing gossip, playing with the children, washing clothes together, dancing at parties, talking politics when the opportunity arose. When the two weeks ended, I recognized ever so clearly my greatest privilege, the option to leave.

Though cotton picking lasted just two short weeks, the memories and the inspiration continue to fill my days. The stack of books by my bed now includes Cardenal, Ortega, Guevara, and Pound (Cardenal's greatest inspiration). My evenings fill up with Spanish language class. My work commitment to food cooperatives diminishes some as I give more and more time to a new business, Equal Exchange,[1] which promises to import and aggressively market high-quality food products from Third World countries, e.g., Nicaraguan coffee.

And my heart beats a little bit in Spanish, with clear images of the puffy white valley between the volcanoes and the sea north of León.

---

[1]Equal Exchange is a new alternative trading organization that seeks to help create a more equitable model of international trade. For more information write to: Equal Exchange, 3 Cambridge Terrace, Allston, Massachusetts 02134.

Gail Gabler

We decided to name ourselves the "Sandy Pollack Peace Brigade." Sandy had the idea to organize people from several antiwar groups, like the Freeze Campaign, the Pledge of Resistance, and the War Resisters League, to volunteer in the Nicaraguan harvest at the same time that the U.S. government was beginning the Big Pine III military maneuvers in Honduras. She was on the flight from Havana to Managua that crashed last January. She was going to Managua to make final arrangements for our brigade when she died. It was a tribute to her.

Less than twenty-four hours after we arrived in Nicaragua, we were picking cotton. We were sent to a farm outside León. We arrived, had a meeting at the ATC office, and cleaned out the rooms where we were going to be staying. The foreman came by and said, okay, we'll show you how to pick in the morning. We said, no, let's start now. So they took us right out and showed us what to do.

We worked with a group of Salvadoran refugees who also had a nearby collective farm. A brigade of students from León also worked on our farm. We were thrilled to learn that Carlos Fonseca's teenage children, Tanya and Carlos, Jr., were part of this brigade. Carlos had been one of the three founders of the FSLN. Tanya had learned to speak English in Cuba, so we got to know her very well. And Carlos, Jr. had been the first person to sign up for the draft when it was announced.

Our best picker was Charles Scott Chapman, from California. He picked 268 pounds one day. That's good for a Nicaraguan and very good for a North American brigadista. Our health responsable was Dr. Ed Manwell from Massachusetts. He was eighty years old, a great doctor, and picked forty pounds a day. He would take the water and say, "Well, this is probably not good for us," and then he would go ahead and have the first drink.

I had lived in Nicaragua for four and a half months in 1983, so after the brigade I went to stay with friends in Managua for several days. At 11:00 PM one night, we heard a series of explosions going off. You get used to guns and explosions when you are there. The kids on the farms would sometimes fire their rifles, even though they're supposed to save all their ammunition. So you don't get fazed. When we began to hear the second and third explosions within ten minutes, we began to wonder.

We went outside and could see smoke rising over the area of the military hospital. Cars were racing down the streets with their lights out, in case it was an air attack. All the soldiers and militia were coming out to their positions in the streets, getting ready. None of them knew what was going on.

We turned on the radio to listen for news. Finally a voice came on: "Atención, atención, atención!" They issued a call for all doctors and medical personnel to report to their stations of work. So then we thought, oh no, this is terrible. People have been hurt and the contras have hit a target in Managua. Finally it was announced that a short circuit had caused the explosions and that no one was killed or seriously hurt. Some medicines, which are in short supply, were destroyed. They had had to evacuate the military hospital, and that was the reason they had mobilized the medical personnel.

We were glad it turned out to be so anticlimactic. But I remember the feeling when the explosion first went off, thinking, "Could this be it? Are the marines coming?" It was impressive to see how quickly the militia was able to mobilize.

Douglas E. Watkin

There is something very special about *working* with people of other countries and cultures. We went to learn of the situation in Nicaragua, but also to work. I'm still emotionally high because of the experience. I'm ready to go again.

Being part of a brigade helped me get in touch with the situation in Nicaragua. My consciousness has been raised to the point that I feel the urgency of involving myself much more in the struggle for peace in Central America.

Returned brigadistas join April 20, 1985 demonstration at the U.S. Capitol protesting Reagan administration policies in Central America. Photo by Daryl Williams.

Postscript

In a speech to the annual meeting of the Conservative Political Action Conference, President Reagan referred to the contras as "our brothers" and "freedom fighters."

"And we owe them our help," he said. "You know the truth about them, and you know who they're fighting and why. They are the moral equal of our Founding Fathers and the brave men and women of the French Resistance."

"We cannot turn away from them," he said. "For the struggle here is not right versus left, but right versus wrong."

New York Times, March 1, 1985

On March 30, 1985, 100 contra entered La Isla de Upa, 35 kilometers northeast of Matagalpa, where 28 North American brigadistas had spent most of January picking coffee with the largely Miskito population of the UPE. Eric Worl, a member of the January 4 brigade who stayed in Nicaragua, sent a report via his family: "On March 30, while I was back visiting La Isla de Upa, someone spotted some contra outside the village. The 400 villagers assembled quickly and without panic, in order to leave. I was the only North American with them. No one in the village was armed. 100 contra came into the village, firing as they came, killing a teenager. They caught up with us outside of town, questioned us, and let us go. We watched as they returned to the village, ransacked every house; then blew up the only truck, the only food store, all the coffee processing equipment and the coffee business office."

Brigadista Bulletin No. 15, May, 1985

Chronology

1522-1524	Conquest of Nicaragua by the Spanish.
1544	Dominican bishop Fray Antonio de Valdivieso arrives in León. For his work defending Nicaragua's native peoples, he is assassinated by an agent of the Spanish crown on February 26, 1550.
1823	U.S. government announces Monroe Doctrine, declaring Latin America to be in its "sphere of influence."
1838	Nicaragua becomes an independent state.
1849	Cornelius Vanderbilt, North American millionaire, obtains concession to build a canal across Nicaragua. It is never completed.
1855	First North American military intervention (non-governmental). An adventurer, William Walker from Tennessee, arrives with fifty-five mercenaries.
1856	William Walker is elected president of Nicaragua, in an unconstitutional election, at the age of thirty-two. The United States officially recognizes his government. Two months after his election, Walker reinstitutes slavery, which had been outlawed when independence

was gained, and declares his intention to join Nicaragua with the southern United States.

1857   Walker is forced out of Nicaragua.

1857-1893   Nicaragua is governed by the conservative party.

1893   General José Santos Zelaya takes power. A liberal reformer, he separates church and state, limits the power and wealth of the Catholic church, and reforms the judiciary.

            When Zelaya begins to reassert Nicaraguan control over the Atlantic coast, tax U.S. investors, and plan to build a canal, the United States severs diplomatic relations.

1895   Augusto Cesar Sandino is born, May 19, in the village of Niquinohomo.

1909   The United States backs a conservative rebellion against Zelaya. U.S. marines intervene. Civil war follows.

1912   Two thousand seven hundred U.S. marines end civil war with a massacre of 600 Nicaraguan supporters of General Benjamin Zeledon.

1921-1925   Sandino works in Honduras and Guatemala for United Fruit Company and then in Mexico for the South Penn Oil Company. He becomes head of the gasoline sales department of the Huasteca Petroleum Company.

            U.S. marines leave Nicaragua, after installing a liberal-conservative alliance in power.

National Guard is created.

1926   Civil war is renewed. Four thousand U.S. troops intervene.

Sandino returns to Nicaragua to fight "Yankee Imperialism" May 16. He sides with liberals in the civil war, rises to the rank of general.

A U.S. government spokesman, justifying intervention, states that Mexico is "...exporting the Bolshevik revolution to the Central American republics...," especially Nicaragua, in order "...to insert a hostile wedge between the United States and the Panama Canal."

1927   U.S. presidential envoy imposes pact on warring parties, including reorganization of National Guard under U.S. control. Pact is opposed by Sandino, who founds the "Army in Defense of National Sovereignty" on September 2.

1927-1932   War between Sandino's army and the United States.

1933   Unable to defeat Sandino, U.S. troops withdraw on January 1. Anastasio Somoza García is placed in charge of the National Guard.

Sandino signs a peace treaty with liberal President Juan Bautista Sacasa on February 2.

1934   Sandino is assassinated by National Guard under the orders of Somoza on February 21.

1935	Carlos Fonseca Amador is born in Matagalpa.
1936	Somoza forces Sacasa to resign and, in an election closely controlled by the National Guard, is elected president by a vote of 107,201 to 169 for his opponent.
1956	Anastasio Somoza García is assassinated by the poet Rigoberto Lopez Perez on September 21. He is succeeded by his son Luis. His younger son, Anastasio Somoza Debayle has already become head of the National Guard.
1959	Cuban Revolution
1961	The United States forms Alliance for Progress. Attempted CIA-Cuban exile invasion of Cuba is defeated at the Bay of Pigs. Landing craft debark for invasion from Nicaragua's east coast.
	Carlos Fonseca, Tomás Borge, and Silvio Mayorga found the FSLN.
1967	Luis Somoza dies. Anastasio Somoza Debayle becomes president of Nicaragua for the 1967-1971 term.
1972	Devastating earthquake rocks Managua in December. As many as 20,000 deaths occur.
1973	Democratically elected socialist government of Salvador Allende is overthrown by Chilean military.
1974	Anastasio Somoza Debayle is reelected with 95 percent of the vote. Under new electoral

law, nine of ten opposition parties are disqualified from participation.

Somoza family wealth estimated to reach 900 million dollars.

FSLN stages major military action, attacking the home of Somoza's agriculture minister during party honoring the U.S. ambassador. FSLN gains the release of political prisoners, including Daniel Ortega Saavedra and José Benito Escobar. Somoza is forced to pay a ransom of 2 million dollars, grant wage increases for workers, and allow the publication of FSLN statements in newspapers and on the radio.

Somoza declares state of seige that lasts for thirty-three months. National Guard begins widespread peasant massacres in an attempt to crush popular support for the Sandinistas.

1976	Tomás Borge and thirteen other Sandinista leaders arrested and tortured. FSLN founder Carlos Fonseca Amador killed in battle on November 8.
1977	Father Fernando Cardenal testifies before a U.S. Congressional subcommittee on peasant massacres by the National Guard in Zelaya.

Twelve leading Nicaraguans (Los Doce), including priests Fernando Cardenal and Miguel D'Escoto and the writer Sergio Ramirez, issue a statement saying there can be no solution to the country's problems without the participation of the FSLN in government and an end to the dictatorship.

1978   Elite National Guard unit formed under the leadership of Anastasio Somoza Debayle's son Anastasio Somoza Portocarrero. Pedro Joaquin Chamorro, publisher of *La Prensa,* is assassinated under orders of Somoza Portocarrero in January. Middle-class opposition to Somoza dictatorship grows.

Partial insurrection in Indian barrio of Monimbo occurs in February.

Somoza is unable to prevent the return to Nicaragua of Los Doce. They are greeted by huge demonstrations.

FSLN commando unit takes over the National Palace in August, winning freedom for political prisoners and other demands, including a minimum wage.

Insurrections occur in seven cities in September. They are put down by the National Guard, which bombs residential areas and markets. U.S. President Carter proposes an "Inter-American Peacekeeping Force."

1979   FSLN begins its final offensive on May 29. Somoza flees to Miami on July 17. National Guard surrenders on July 19. FSLN military units enter Managua and join with urban insurrection.

The cost of victory is high: 50,000 are dead; 200,000 families are homeless; 40,000 children are orphaned; a third of all industry is destroyed. Somoza leaves a foreign debt of 1.6 billion dollars; and 3.5 million dollars are left in the national treasury.

FSLN organizes Junta of National Reconstruction. Property of Somoza and his allies is confiscated and nationalized: 1.2 million acres, half the cultivatable land in Nicaragua. Banks and all natural resources, especially the mines, are nationalized.

The Somoza legacy: 50.2 percent of Nicaraguans are illiterate; 70 percent have no access to medical attention; 20 percent of all children die before reaching the age of four.

FSLN launches literacy campaign. Over 100,000 young people participate. Illiteracy is reduced to 12 percent in less than ten months.

1980   Anastasio Somoza Debayle is assassinated in Paraguay on September 17, by Argentinian revolutionaries.

Ronald Reagan is elected president of the United States, winning votes from slightly more than 26 percent of the U.S. electorate.

FSLN issues statement on religion, pledging total freedom of belief, expression, and practice and recognizing the role of Christians in the struggle for liberation and their right to membership in the FSLN.

1981   CIA begins "covert" war against Nicaragua. There are 158 violations of Nicaraguan air space and land. The U.S. training of former

National Guardsmen begins in the United States.

1982   Reagan destabilization plan proceeds. Attacks on economic targets inside Nicaragua begin. Divisions among the Central American countries are fomented. Honduras is converted into a military base and sanctuary for the contras, who are lodged near the Nicaraguan border, trained by foreign advisers, supplied with modern weapons, and organized into military units to penetrate Nicaraguan territory.

1983   Pope John Paul II visits Nicaragua in March. Eight hundred thousand people attend open-air mass.

Nicaragua expels three U.S. diplomats, accusing them of plotting to poison Foreign Minister Miguel D'Escoto. The U.S. government retaliates by closing all Nicaraguan consulates in the United States except Washington, D.C., and denying landing rights to all Aeronica flights except at Miami airport.

CIA-led contras fail in attempt to seize part of Nicaraguan territory in order to create a provisional government and request U.S. aid.

The oil storage facility at Corinto is destroyed by a CIA-led commando attack on October 10. Oil tanks burn for several days and 27,000 people are evacuated.

An underwater pipeline at Puerto Sandino is sabotaged on October 14.

The United States launches Big Pine II, military maneuvers in Honduras involving nineteen war ships with 16,484 crewmen and 6,000 ground troops.

The Caribbean island of Grenada is invaded by U.S. military, and its revolutionary government is ousted.

1984   CIA-led commandos mine Nicaraguan ports and bomb Nicaraguan territory. A secret CIA document lists nineteen such operations in the first months of 1984 (*Wall Street Journal*, March 5, 1985).

Nicaragua sues the United States for violations against its territory in the International Court of Justice (the World Court).

Secretary of State George Shultz visits Managua on June 1. On the same day, contras attack Ocotál, destroying a granary, a lumber mill, silos, and coffee warehouses. Many are killed and wounded during two-day battle.

Democratic presidential candidate Jesse Jackson visits Nicaragua at the end of June.

1985   President Reagan announces on January 18 that the United States will refuse to take part in further World Court proceedings in Nicaragua's suit.

The United States launches Big Pine III.

In the United States, more than 100,000 people participate in nation-wide demonstrations against U.S. military intervention in Central America, April 20.

On May 1, President Reagan states that "the policies and actions of the Nicaraguan government constitute an unusual and extraordinary threat to the national security and foreign policy of the United States" and declares a national emergency. He imposes an embargo on trade between the United States and Nicaragua.

Index

About the Contributors

Victoria Alba, thirty, is a photojournalist from San Francisco, California. She is of Filipino-Mexican-Apache ancestry and writes for *El Tecolote*, a bilingual community newspaper.

Rikki Asher, twenty-nine, is an arts educator at a public junior high school in the Bronx, New York.

Bill Bailey was working as a union organizer when the Spanish Civil War broke out in 1936. Outraged at the U.S. government policy of nonintervention that prohibited the shipment of arms to the Republican Loyalists and banned travel to Spain, he joined with others from the United States to form the Abraham Lincoln Brigade. This unpaid and nonprofessional troop of men and women chose to fight the Fascists with the International Brigade alongside the Republican Loyalists. Bill Bailey has recently been seen in two movies: "Seeing Red," about the history of the U.S. Communist Party, and "The Good Fight," about the history of the Abraham Lincoln Brigade.

Betty Bishop, fifty-three, is a painter from Berkeley, California.

Annie Borgenicht is a delivery room nurse from San Francisco, California. She is currently working with the Committee for Health Rights in Central America (CHRICA), a training project for Nicaraguan nurses, and nurse auxiliaries in maternity nursing and maternal/child health.

Jim Calder, thirty-two, is an actor from New York City.

Lisa Christensen, twenty, is a baker and copartner in an art gallery specializing in crafts from Sonoma County, California.

Earl Christy, thirty-two, is a union construction laborer from Charleston, West Virginia.

Andrew Courtney, forty-eight, is a high school teacher from Mount Kisco, New York.

Kathleen Donahoe, thirty-nine, is a bookkeeper in Colville, Washington.

Neil Dunaetz, thirty, is a self-employed wholesaler of used railroad ties to lumber companies and garden centers. He lives in Chicago, Illinois.

Steve Emerman, twenty-eight, is a Post-Doctoral Associate in Geo-Physics at Cornell University, Ithaca, New York.

Janet Essley, thirty-six, is a tree planter and migrant worker in the Pacific Northwest.

Antonio Flores is foreman of UPE Aracely Ramirez Tapia, El Crucero, Nicaragua.

Sesshu Foster, twenty-seven, is a writer and poet. He is a teaching assistant in East Los Angeles, California. His antecedents were landless farmers from the U.S. Midwest and Hiroshima Province, Japan. Half of his family spent World War II in concentration camps in the Arizona desert.

Richard W. Franke is Professor of Anthropology at Montclair State College, Upper Montclair, New Jersey.

Gail Gabler, twenty-six, is a union organizer and secretary from Brooklyn, New York.

Kevin Gerien is a photojournalist from New York City.

Gwendolyn Gilliam, thirty, is a burlesque dancer and writer. She is coauthor of *Accidental Killers*, a study of how people cope with accidentally taking a human life. She lives in Berkeley, California.

Paul Griffin, twenty-nine, is an artist and carpenter from New Paltz, New York.

Brenda Grove, thirty, is a counselor of deaf-retarded adults from Minneapolis, Minnesota.

Joan Harmon, thirty-one, is an artist and carpenter from New York City.

Jeff Jones, thirty-eight, is a printer and writer. He was an active opponent of the U.S. war against Vietnam and is currently working on a history of the Student Non-Violent Coordinating Committee (SNCC). He lives in New York City with Eleanor Stein and their two children, Thai and Arthur.

Thai Stein Jones, eight, is a third grader in a New York City public school and would like to go to Nicaragua.

James W. Lahey, forty-four, is a writer and auto mechanic, and was a Green Beret in the Vietnam War.

Reverend Kathryn Lee is a Director for Parish Support for the American Lutheran Church. She lives in St. Paul, Minnesota.

Reverend Otis Lee is Minister at Christ's Lutheran Church, St. Paul, Minnesota.

Barbara Leon, forty, is a writer and office worker. She is active in the Mid-Hudson Valley Nicaragua Support Project and the Coalition Against Apartheid and Racism in New Paltz, New York.

Richard Levy, thirty-nine, lives in Boston, Massachusetts, where he teaches English as a second language to adult Chinese immigrants.

Margaret Lobenstine, forty-two, runs a bed and breakfast country inn in Ware, Massachusetts. She is married and has twin daughters about to enter college.

Suzanne Marten, twenty-three, recently graduated from New York University. She is currently working with Nicaragua Exchange.

Sara Miles is a poet and political activist. She is a staff member of Nicaragua Exchange and has spent the past two years organizing harvest brigades to Nicaragua.

Kit Miller, thirty, is Associate Project Director of the Central America T.V. Organizing Project in San Francisco, California.

Ric Mohr, twenty-eight, is a seasonal farm worker, artist, and teacher in Putney, Vermont.

Sister Sheila Murphy, fifty-three, is Principal of Our Lady of Mercy Elementary School in the Bronx, New York.

Elaine Myrianthopoulos is a day care teacher and political activist from New York City.

Eugene Novogrodsky, forty-six, is a former news and sports reporter from Manchester, Vermont. He is married, has two children, and is currently working as a concrete laborer.

Judith Holton Rew, thirty-one, is a free-lance graphic artist who lives in New York City.

Joe Richey, twenty-seven, is Executive Director of the Maine Writers and Publishers Alliance. He lives in Portland, Maine.

Anne Rodman is a nurse practitioner from Fox River, Oregon. She was overall health coordinator for the 1984–1985 harvest brigades and also worked with the reforestation and construction brigades.

Michael Rozyne, twenty-eight, is manager of Equal Exchange, an alternative trading organization in Concord, Massachusetts.

Victor Sanchez is a photojournalist from New York City.

Gail Sangree, fifty, is a community college instructor from Watertown, Connecticut.

Suzanne Sangree is a law student in Queens, New York. She is cofounder of Casa Nicaragüense de Español and has lived in Nicaragua.

Shana Saper lives in Montreal, Canada.

Audrey Seniors, forty-four, is a Black woman and the mother of a twenty-two-year-old daughter. She has been a political activist for nearly twenty-five years. She works as a legal secretary at the Center for Constitutional Rights in New York City.

Sofia Sequenzia, thirty-six, is a librarian from Brooklyn, New York.

Maxine Shaw, thirty-nine, is a public school teacher from Brookline, Massachusetts. She has two sons. She is currently working for a year in Nicaragua for the Ministry of Education.

Judith Anne Singer is a union organizer from Milwaukee, Wisconsin.

Zachary Sklar, thirty-six, is a writer and editor and teaches at Columbia School of Journalism in New York City.

Willie Sordill, thirty-four, is a secretary and musician from Cambridge, Massachusetts.

Teresa Sosa, twenty, is a biracial Latina. She is a part-time college student from New York City.

Sox Sperry, thirty-two, is a teacher and political activist from Fort Wayne, Indiana.

Jeffry Steele is a musician and teacher from Cambridge, Massachusetts.

Eleanor Stein, thirty-nine, is a writer and law student in New York City. She was an organizer against the Vietnam War and has two children.

Joyce Stoller, thirty-five, is a writer from San Francisco, California.

Rosemarie Straijer, twenty-four, is a singer and Manager of the Underground Railway Theater.

John Strong, forty-nine, is a professor of history and American studies at the Southampton Center of C.W. Post College, Southampton, New York.

Becky Thorne is a journalist who works with radio station WBAI in New York City.

Paul Tick, thirty-one, is a social worker and photographer. He works with New Jewish Agenda's National Task Force on Central America.

Wendy Wallas, thirty-five, is a graphic artist from Putney, Vermont.

Douglas E. Watkin, thirty-seven, is a dairy farmer from Oriskany Falls, New York.

Lois Wessel, twenty-two, is a tenant organizer and swimming instructor, currently working in Nicaragua as a translator. She is from New Haven, Connecticut.

Daryl Williams is a tour guide and photographer from New York City.

Debra Wise, thirty-two, is Co-Director of the Underground Railway Theater from Cambridge, Massachusetts.

Morris Wright, seventy-seven, is a staff writer for *Frontline*. For more than twenty years, he was editor of *The Union,* the newspaper of the International Union of Mine, Mill, and Smelter Workers (which merged with the United States Steel Workers in 1967). He lives in Oakland, California.

Anthony Yarus is a printer and photojournalist from New York City.